A Learning Ideabook™

Inventors Workshop

by Alan J. McCormack

Fearon Teacher Aids, a division of **David S. Lake Publishers**   Belmont, California

TO SUSAN
Without her this book
would have remained
an impossible dream.

OTHER TITLES IN THE CRAFTS WORKSHOP SERIES:

MAKE YOUR OWN GAMES WORKSHOP
NATIVE AMERICAN CRAFTS WORKSHOP
NATURE CRAFTS WORKSHOP
TRASH ARTISTS WORKSHOP

Editorial director: Roberta Suid
Editor: Bonnie Bernstein
Production manager: Patricia Clappison
Design manager: Eleanor Mennick
Designer: Jane Mitchell
Illustrator: Duane Bibby
Cover designer: William Nagel

ISBN–0-8224-9783-2
Library of Congress Card Catalog Number: 80-84185
Printed in the United States of America.

1.9 8 7 6 5

Preface

Inventors Workshop features more than twenty-five challenging projects and activities appropriate for kids in elementary and junior high school. The book is designed for use by teachers in the classroom or by parents who would like to work with their children on enjoyable, inventive science projects at home. Some kids—gifted children, in particular—will want to use the book independently or with a minimum of adult supervision as a source of ideas for science fair projects, and as a vehicle for personal challenge and enrichment.

A few of the activities require only this book, paper and a pencil, and a willing imagination. Most, however, involve kids in the construction of an intriguing invention or scientific device. Though plans for building a particular device are provided in most activities, the initial construction should be considered only a springboard for further discovery. A number of Inventive Sidetrips follow each project challenging kids to test their inventiveness by modifying existing devices or building originals. Hints and helpful information for solving these challenges are provided in a section called Inventors Notes and Solutions.

True science begins when a person sees a problem that seems challenging and devises his or her own means for solving it. This inventive process can be exciting and frustrating, satisfying and confounding—just like all of humankind's most important activities.

Happy inventing!

Contents

Introduction for Teachers and Parents

According to recent magazine and newspaper articles, America is losing its edge on the rest of the world in innovation and invention. Some journalists have dubbed this situation "the innovation gap."

Experts blame this problem on everything from inflation eating up research and development budgets to depletion of natural resources and outmoded industrial facilities. Too often they overlook the integral fact that new ideas don't come from dollars, complex machines, or ultramodern facilities, but from people. The imagination of people is the one natural resource we have that can't become too expensive, depleted, or outmoded. Creativity and imagination will always be the keys to hope for the future, no matter how bleak or problem-ridden is the present.

Major contributors to the innovation gap may very well be schools and society in general. Schools and social institutions tend to encourage and reward knowledge of science and society's past achievements and sound skills in reading, writing, and arithmetic, but not in imagination. Some recent medical research on the function of the human brain makes neglect of the imagination seem almost criminal.

On direct observation, the two halves of the human brain look like mirror images of each other. They weigh about the same and have the same shape. But they don't function in the same way, perceive the same things, or operate in the same cognitive arenas.

The outer, and bulkiest, part of the brain is called the cerebrum, and it consists of left and right hemispheres. Many researchers now believe the left hemisphere is predominantly involved with linear, logical, sequential thought—it is the site of ordered reason. The right hemisphere functions in visual or spatial relations, artistic talents, imagination, synthesis of new ideas, intuition, and other nonsequential mind functions. The left hemisphere is the practical logician; the right is the dreamer, the artist, the inventor.

In Western society, especially in the sciences, it seems that the left brain hemisphere dominates the right. Logic and analysis seem legitimate thinking skills, while fantasy and oddball inventiveness are kept closeted in our minds' attics.

All of this would seem to have important implications for both formal schooling and for informal education of children by their parents. You might categorize much of our system of education as half-brained, as it tends to ignore one whole half of the brain. This can leave one-half of the child's mental potential relatively undeveloped.

This is not to say that in school programs or in education in the home we should strive for predominantly right-brained learning and thinking. Moving entirely in that direction would be just as great an injustice to kids as maintaining our traditional left-brained approach. The highest achievements of humankind have been brought about by synergy—the complementary workings of our two modes of thought in which the combination of the two is greater than the sum of the parts.

A look at the work of creative scientists such as Einstein reveals that intuitive visualization, reverie, and unstructured dreaming typically precede the development of a great new idea. That is, right brain activity seems to come first. Once a new idea is created, then it is further refined, tested, and made practical by the logical mechanisms of the left brain. So we need to communicate to youngsters that both modes of thought have value and are vital to innovation in any field of endeavor.

But we generally have not done this. Paul Torrance, in a study of thousands of young children, found considerable creative abilities in children at about age four and one-half—just before they enter school. A gradual increase in creativity can then be observed until age nine, where a plateau is reached. After this point, research findings on creative thinking can be summarized in one statement: *If you don't use it, you lose it.*

That brings us to what this book is all about—projects parents and teachers can use with youngsters to provide experiences with the playful, imaginative, and inventive facets of their minds. The projects are designed so that they can be accomplished by individual youngsters or groups of youngsters, either at home or as part of a school science program. Elements of mystery, illusion, humor, and fantasy are combined with basic scientific principles to entice kids to do things that come naturally to them: play with ideas; dream; take gadgets apart; build oddball contraptions; and have fun.

The projects in this book are all designed to encourage creative, right-hemispheric thinking. Since the book focuses on the areas of science and invention, three mental processes will be given greatest emphasis: a) visual thinking; b) inventive thinking; and c) humor.

VISUAL THINKING

Visual thinking is also known as imagery. It is, put simply, the process of seeing pictures in the mind's eye. Visual thinking is one of the more predominant and important right-hemispheric processes, yet it also has been one of the most neglected by designers of learning activities for children.

Imagine trying to develop a new scientific idea—or even read—without mentally picturing things. Testimonies from Archimedes, Kekule, Faraday, Newton, Einstein and a legion of other significant thinkers attest that one thing can be found in common in all discoveries: thinking in images. Many of the projects in this book will enable a parent or teacher to provide enjoyable and worthwhile ways kids can tune up their visual thinking skills—and enjoy doing it.

INVENTIVE THINKING

Inventive thinking requires improvisation. The thinker needs to imagine unique ways of looking at common objects, of developing uncommon uses for them, and of changing or transforming these objects in new ways. Flexibility and originality are the essence of inventive thinking.

At the core of inventive thinking is the capacity to see the commonplace as strange. All of us have been left-brain educated since childhood to categorize the world into traditional, convenient units and to use the accepted labels for these units. Soon the categories and labels become sacred and immutable, and we tend to view things around us in a rigid way. Those who retain the ability to overcome this rigidity are able to produce new ideas much more often than those who do not. For example:

"What uses can you think of for a tin can?"

"To preserve vegetables in, or use it as a pencil holder."

"And?"

"And? That's what tin cans are for!"

"Sorry friend, you display all the symptoms of rigid, overly constrained, and convergent thinking. I'm afraid you suffer from a common ailment—functional fixation."

"From what?!"

"Look at it this way: if you weren't bound by your fixation, you might realize that a tin can could be used as a birdhouse, a wagon wheel, a yarn winder, or a worm guard for your tomato plants. An elongated can might make a dandy rolling pin, umbrella holder, or table leg. Or a can cut lengthwise could be a shoe scraper, a scoop, or a rocking toy base. And don't forget their possibilities as cookie cutters, bongo drums, or measuring devices."

Profound effects can come from a very simple change in the way you look at an object or situation. Edison used this trick when he invented the Gramophone. He turned unwanted recorded background noise from a telegraph into an astonishingly accurate reproduction of sound. The cash register was conceived when Jack Ritty was watching a device that counted the revolutions of a ship's propeller. Eli Whitney got the idea for his cotton gin when he saw a solution in the claws of a cat to the problem of stripping cotton from cotton plants.

One of the keys to the invention process is the realization that new inventions are almost never really new. They are made from known objects that already exist in nature, combined in new ways. All inventive developments are built on previous ones. The axe, for example, combines the principles of the lever and the knife. A few mechanical principles, known for centuries, were brought together in a radical new combination to perfect the rotary can opener. It made a fortune for its inventor. For Edison, the technologies for making sealed glass containers, developing partial vacuums, and constructing electrical circuits were already well known. When he invented the light bulb, his genius was in seeing in these a relationship that had not occurred to others.

Raw materials for inventive thinking are all around us. Cardboard, coat hangers, old jars, string, and other miscellaneous junk are invaluable to the process. There is great credence in the "Theory of Loose Parts," which postulates that the degree of creativeness by children in any environment is directly proportional to the number and diversity of objects available in the environment. Couple this theory with one of the "Ten Commandments for Inventors"—"Thou shalt scrounge"—and you've got it: boxes of enticing junk just begging to be combined into new inventions.

When you try some of the activities in this book with youngsters, you will find that kids are quite good at generating ideas. Children haven't experienced enough of life to be brainwashed by the usual way-things-should-be-done attitude nor are they concerned with the business person's continuing battle with time, cost, and materials. And, because they have flexible minds still fascinated with the wonder of simple things, they can be impressive, creative inventors.

HUMOR

Creativity is commonly thought of as a serious business. Inventors are conceived of as somber recluses fixated with building the "Ultimate Time and Labor Saver." Artists are pictured in humorless pursuit of "The Great Masterpiece." Obviously, there can be no time for frivolousness when a person is in the throes of creative thought.

You may be surprised to learn that these stereotypes are largely untrue. Humor, creativity researchers have found, is very frequently associated with creative processes and personalities. Psychologists have explored the relationships among humor, insight, and creative thinking and found these to be closely related processes. Creative thinking is an insight process: it involves a switch from an ordinary or conventional way of looking at a situation to one that is better. In other words, creativity is essentially looking at things in a different way that is better than the ordinary way. Humor often involves a similar process of seeing a situation in a new or unusual way. The new way of viewing a situation becomes humorous when it is bizarre, exaggerated, or a violation of natural laws of nature or society.

It is interesting that the single trait frequently found to characterize highly creative students is not high scores on I.Q. tests. The one trait these gifted students generally have in common is a sense of humor! This observation further supports the idea that creative insight and humor are closely related mental processes. And both of these mental functions should be encouraged.

Production of humor is a creative process much like the production of a new invention. Both involve a kind of flexibility and divergence of thinking enabling the thinker to perceive things in a unique way. Purposeful use of learning activities involving humor can be motivating, socially lubricating, and a good way to open up perceptions and receptiveness to new ideas. That's why many of the projects featured in this book have a humorous quality.

Now it's up to you. Most kids won't become Edisons or Newtons merely because they have participated in science activities involving inventive, visual, and imaginative thinking. But they can learn to produce new ideas—even to delight in them. And they can learn that solving problems isn't something always to be left for the other guy. Creativity can become a way of life!

Introduction for Young Inventors

Some people see things as they are and ask why;
I dream of things that never were and ask why not.
(Traditional Motto of Inventors)

So you want to be an inventor? Great! This book can help you. Like any other skill, inventing can be learned. And, the more you practice, the better you become at it.

The first thing you will need to do is develop an inventor's frame of mind; it's a can-do or let's-try-it-and-see way of life that views inventing and constructing scientific projects as sports, rather than hard work or someone else's problem.

To be creative (which, of course, is an inventor's main asset) you will need to train yourself to see everyday objects in new ways. When you see a brick, for example, don't think of it as a block for building walls—that's what everyone else sees. Instead, think of that brick as a boat anchor, a paperweight, a target for hoop games, an exercise weight or a knife sharpener. Never again think of it as a plain old brick. Creative people, like yourself and professional inventors, are always able to see multiple possibilities for using any object.

Another inventor's skill you should practice is the process of seeing in your mind's eye—that is, visualizing pictures in your mind. Inventors are skilled at clearly imagining how objects might look if they were combined in some way. They are also good at mentally picturing the hidden innards of gadgets and machines. This special kind of imagination is called *visual thinking,* and it is a skill worth practicing.

Of course, inventing is easier if you also develop some skills with your hands. Connections between wood, wire, tin cans, and cardboard require some basic skills of cutting, gluing, bolting, and painting—but these are easily learned and can be a lot of fun.

Finally—are you ready for this? Here is the great secret of invention: *inventions are almost never entirely new!* They are combinations of already existing objects and ideas put together in a new way or for a new purpose. Take scissors, for example. This is how they were invented: two knives were connected by a pivot and the knives' straight handles were replaced by finger rings. Ingenious at the time—but all the ingredients were already well known and waiting for someone to put them together in just the right way. Think of the possibilities! You can invent all sorts of gadgets by combining everyday things in new ways. Remember, Frisbees were inspired by pie tins and hot air balloons were invented when a paper maker was burning some unwanted paper bags. Always be on the lookout for new uses of objects, or unusual combinations of them.

A final word of advice—scrounge! Scrounge for ideas you can improve on or modify. Search in newspapers, magazines, and books for problems to be solved, new gadgets and products, and new scientific discoveries. Ask yourself: What other possibilities do these suggest?" Also, scrounge for all kinds of odd objects. Every inventor's workshop

needs a stockpile of raw materials for making inventions. Once you
have found space in your locker, the garage, or a spare classroom or
bedroom closet, venture out on a scavenger hunt to collect discarded,
broken, or unwanted materials, parts, and mechanical pieces that
might prove useful. The list below offers some possibilities, but you'll
find others. And, as you scrounge around, remember: Yesterday's junk
may become tomorrow's great invention!

SCROUNGE LIST

Milk cartons
Empty thread spools
Tin cans
Toothpicks
Glasses, bottles
Safety pins
Paper clips
Lubricating oil
Baking soda
Lids
Glue
Sandwich bags
Salt
Eggs
Nails
Yarn
Combs
Foil
Waxed paper
Plexiglass
Scrap lumber and plywood
Pins
Dowels
Candles
Old pots
Worn out electrical
    appliances
Ice cream buckets
Tubing (plastic or rubber)
Eye droppers
Cardboard and pasteboard
Ball-point pens
Carpet scraps
Pulleys
Hooks

Film cans
Tinker toys
Nuts & bolts
Popsicle sticks
Paper sacks
Beads, old jewelry
Broken toys
Old plumbing parts
Leather
Paper plates
Cigar boxes
Feathers
Tape
Tools, all types
Screws
Sheet metal
Mirrors
Flashlight batteries & bulbs
Wire
String
Sand
Balloons
Brads
Newspaper
Wire screen
Empty boxes
Coat hangers
Garbage bags
Magnets
Food coloring
Tacks
Material scraps
Springs
Sandpaper

Plastic wrap
Rubber bands
Any parts of old machines
Brass paper fasteners
Packaging materials
Rulers
Nylons, panty hose
Old dishes
Paper towel roll cores
Plastic/paper straws
Old garden hose
Fishing line
Bricks
Timer
Vinegar
Buttons
Spring-type clothespins
Foil pie pans
Ball bearings
Wheels
Old cameras
Tea strainers
Plastic bag fasteners
Washers
Marbles
Paint brushes
Plastic tableware
Yardsticks
Wax
Shoelaces
Toothbrushes
Knobs
Pipes (metal or plastic)
Modeling clay

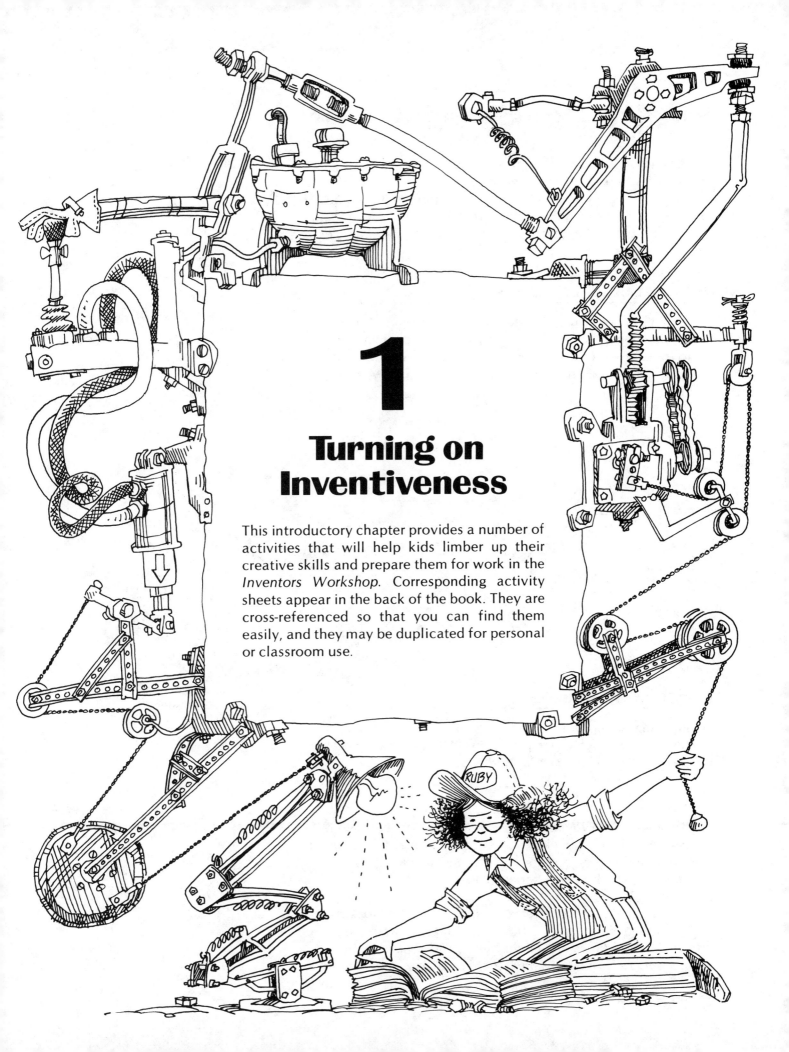

1

Turning on Inventiveness

This introductory chapter provides a number of activities that will help kids limber up their creative skills and prepare them for work in the *Inventors Workshop*. Corresponding activity sheets appear in the back of the book. They are cross-referenced so that you can find them easily, and they may be duplicated for personal or classroom use.

Potato Possibilities

There can be a lot more to potatoes than french fries, hash browns, and chips. Leave it to the imagination of kids and their ability to see the unusual in the usual—potatoes can become some very astonishing things! Here are two introductory exercises that will turn the ordinary potato into an extraordinary experience.

■ NEW AND UNUSUAL POTATOES

The activity sheet on page 73 features four drawings of potatoes—plain, old potatoes. It's the responsibility of an inventive kid to transform those potatoes into something very different—something never before conceived in a potato. Here's an example:

■ POTATO FANTASY TRIP

Seeing things in the mind's eye is essential to the invention process. One way for kids to practice such thinking in pictures is to take a guided fantasy trip. Here's how it's done:

PROCEDURE

1. While you close your eyes and concentrate, have someone read the following out loud to you. The room should be quiet during the fantasy journey, and the reader should pause for about 5 seconds at each series of dots.

    Close your eyes and relax. . . . Imagine you are looking at a large white wall. . . . Try to see a huge brown potato on the wall. . . . Notice the bumps and dents on the potato. . . . Now imagine touching its skin—how does it feel? . . . Now make the potato become super huge—as big as a bus. . . . Imagine yourself crawling on the surface of this monster potato. . . . Take a shovel and dig a tunnel into the potato. . . .

Crawl inside and taste the white potato meat. . . . Imagine the taste of the raw potato. . . . Now continue tunneling until you completely bore through to the other side. . . . Walk away from the potato and look at it once again. . . . Now make it change. . . . First its shape . . . then, its color . . . until it is no longer a potato. . . . Keep in mind what you change it into. . . . Now come back to this room and open your eyes.

2. After completing the fantasy journey, think about your imaginary experiences with the potato. Were you able to picture the huge potato in your mind? How did the raw potato taste? What was it like inside the potato? What did the potato finally change into?

   The more vividly you can picture things and changes in things in your mind, the easier it will be for you to create inventions. Your imagination is one of your most precious assets.

■ INVENTIVE SIDETRIPS

1. Test your powers of observation. Obtain 5–10 raw potatoes and choose one to examine as closely as you can. Be familiar with its every detail. Now, blindfold yourself and have someone mix your potato with the others. Through your mental image of the potato and your sense of touch, see if you can identify the potato. (You may want to write an identifying mark on the potato.)
2. Make a list of as many uses as you can think of for a potato. For example, a potato might be hollowed out and used as a soup bowl. Try to invent uses no one else would think up.
3. Take a raw potato and combine it with other materials to make a model of a new creature. You can paint it with poster paint or color it with felt-tip markers. Perhaps it might resemble a creature from another planet—especially if you leave it in a cool, dark place and let it sprout.

Brainstorms

When people come up with exceptionally good, original ideas, they are often described as having had a *brainstorm*. Scientists who study the process of thinking that enables inventors to dream up new ideas call this process *brainstorming*. Everybody, especially inventors, should get into the creative habit of brainstorming. It's simple, fun, and effective.

Whether people are trying to produce ideas independently or as part of a group, brainstorming is a freewheeling game of collecting ideas based on three simple rules:

☐ Accept and record all ideas that come to mind. Reserve judgment or criticism of ideas for a later time.
☐ Try to produce a large number of ideas, rather than just a few good ideas. The greater the number of ideas (even silly ones), the better the chance of producing winners.
☐ Try to dream up wild or way-out ideas. Often these can be turned into good practical ideas.

Kids should give brainstorming a try using an object from their inventor's junk collection for inspiration.

MATERIALS

Personal collection of junk (see the Scrounge List, page xi)
Pencil with eraser
Paper

PROCEDURE

1. Select any one object from your inventor's materials collection (otherwise known as your junk box). Take 5–10 minutes and list all the ideas you can think of for uses of the object (be sure to apply the three rules of brainstorming).
2. After you have completed your idea list, look it over. Which ideas seem most useful? Psychologists have found that many original ideas occur way down on the list after all the common ideas have been suggested. They also have discovered that oddball ideas are often good stepping stones to other useful ideas.

Combine and Conquer

New inventions are almost never entirely new. They are combinations of objects that already exist. This mental construction activity requires kids to carefully examine the workings of mechanical devices, then use their brainstorming skills to combine the functions of several very different devices so that they perform a new function together. This is not only fun to do, it's inventive!

MATERIALS

Personal collection of junk (see the Scrounge List, page xi)
Pencil with eraser
Paper (or use the form on page 74)

PROCEDURE

1. Without looking, reach inside a box or bag filled with items from your junk collection. Take out three different items.
2. At first, the three objects may seem to have no relationship to each other. Take a few minutes and picture the three objects in your mind's eye. Think about their functions—what they can do, how they work. Then try to make mental pictures of how these three items could be used together to accomplish a new task.
3. When you have come up with a combination, sketch your idea in action. Show how, when combined, your three objects can be used to do a job.

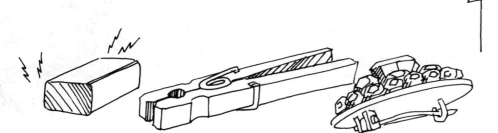

■ INVENTIVE SIDETRIPS

1. Borrow some household gadgets (eggbeater, can opener, pliers, and so on). Examine these and try to identify the simpler parts each gadget is made from. For example: scissors = 2 knives + 2 finger rings + pivot attachment.
2. Take your three original objects apart and try to combine them in such a way that they can actually perform the job you illustrated in your sketch.

Thingamajigs

Believe it or not, *Webster's Dictionary* defines *thingamajig* as a synonym for *thingamabob!* The definition given for thingamabob is only a little more helpful: "any device; a contrivance; a gadget" . . . you know what they mean—a sort of—well . . . a thingamajig! Perhaps this poem might help:

THINGAMAJIG*

What on earth is a thingamajig?
Small and blue? Red and big?
Can you use it on Mondays to brush your teeth?
Is it made of cardboard with springs underneath?

Did you see someone use one while painting a wall?
Was it made from balloons and a squashed rubber ball?
A thingamajig could be heavy or light,
Something to use to make the world bright.

A tiny contraption to catch a gray mouse,
Or an elephant scrubber as big as a house.
Make it from any old junk that you find;
A thingamajig grows in your mind!

Kids must imagine the wildest thingamajig ever—then collect some odds and ends and build it. A thingamajig can be given all sorts of imagined capabilities: for instance, a laser beam producer might have a dye attachment that could color the moon green; another thingamajig might be able to produce happy pills (give one each day to a sourpuss!).

MATERIALS

Personal collection of junk (see the Scrounge List, page xi)
Tape, string, nails, or glue

CONSTRUCTION

1. Assemble a variety of junk materials. You also may need some tape, string, nails, or glue to attach parts of your thingamajig together.
2. Play with fitting the junk objects together in different ways while trying (at the same time) to develop an idea of what your thingamajig might be. Soon, an idea will strike you.
3. Build your thingamajig. Improve it and make it more complicated as you put it together. Remember: Your thingamajig doesn't really have to work—you can simply pretend that various parts of your contraption can do certain things.

*Alan J. McCormack, "Thingamajig," *Learning Magazine,* January 1976, p. 74.

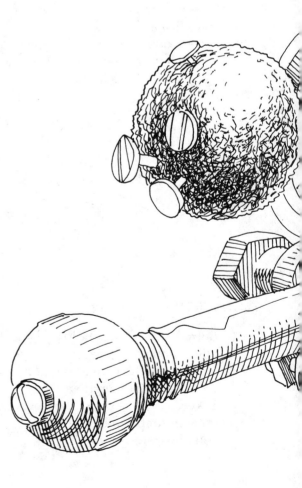

■ INVENTIVE SIDETRIPS

1. Some drawings of thingamajigs that were actually given U.S. patents or manufactured are provided on an activity sheet on page 75. In the spaces provided on the sheet, write out your guesses about the possible uses for each gadget. (The actual intended uses for each are given in Inventors Notes and Solutions on page 64.)

2. Go on a thingamajig hunt. Visit attics, basements, junk yards, your grandparents' garage, or any other likely place, and find unusual mechanical devices. Photographs can be made of the devices, or you may be able to collect some of the actual devices (people are often happy to give them away). The uses for some of the thingamajigs you find may not be known, so try to figure out what the intended uses may have been.

3. Make a collection of photographs and drawings of thingamajigs. Cut pictures from old magazines, newspapers, and catalogues. You might want to sort your pictures into categories: Useless Thingamajigs, Funny Thingamajigs, Energy-Saving Thingamajigs, Energy-Wasting Thingamajigs, Thingamajigs I Would Like to Own.

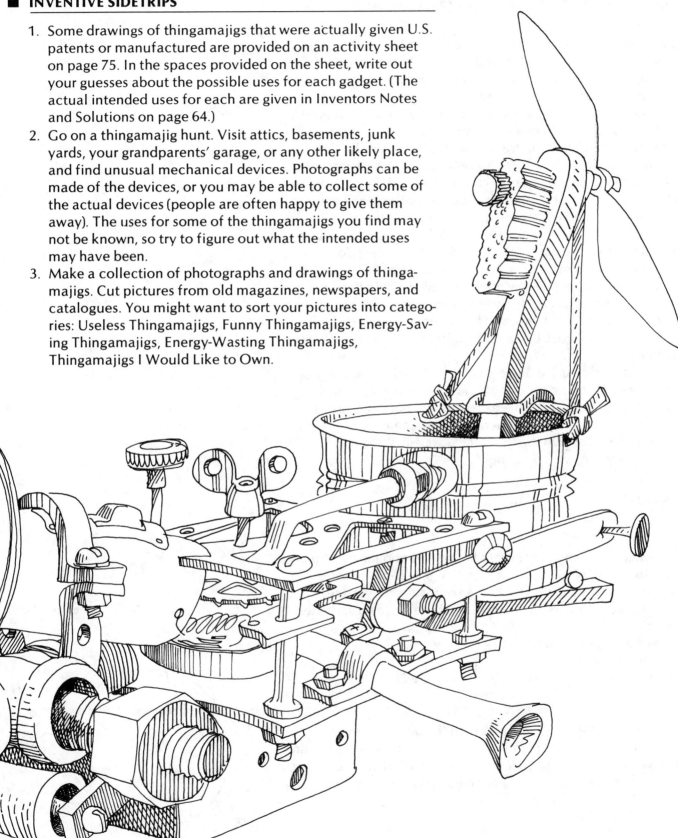

Invention Dissection

Part of an amateur inventor's training should include learning as much as possible about how existing inventions work. Kids can apply the mechanical principles they learn from studying other inventions to designing their own inventions.

It's not hard to find worn-out, broken, or simply unwanted inventions to study. Old clocks, electric egg beaters, toasters, and other mechanical delights are tossed into trash cans by the dozens each day. All of these household gadgets represent the brainstorm of some past creative inventor, and they all incorporate marvelous engineering principles. So, collect one or more of these unwanted jewels and carefully dissect them—take the things apart to see what makes them tick. Dissection is an appropriate word because to the biologist this process does not mean hacking animals to pieces. It means carefully separating the organs of preserved specimens for the purpose of precisely studying them. Kids can apply the same exacting approach to the dissection of machines, and learn about their parts in the same way a biologist becomes familiar with the organs inside animals.

Dissecting discarded devices can be a lot of fun and it provides good experience in using hand tools and in approaching a task systematically. And, the experience of putting a dissected invention back together is much like using logic to solve a puzzle. Are you ready, Doctor? Scalpel . . . scissors. Oops! I mean . . . screwdriver . . . wrench!

MATERIALS

Old newspapers
Old rags
Discarded mechanical gadget (a household appliance such as a
    toaster, iron, blender, clock, fan, or eggbeater—or some
    other unwanted gizmo such as an old lawn mower, electric
    motor, automotive fuel pump or carburetor, lawn sprinkler,
    or bicycle)
Screwdriver, pliers, wrenches
Pencil with eraser
Paper for list (you can use the form on page 76) or a large piece
    of drawing paper to place parts on

Note for kids: Be sure you check with the owner of whatever gadget you choose for permission to take it apart. Also, be sure to have your parents or your teacher know what you plan to do so they can make sure there are no dangers involved.

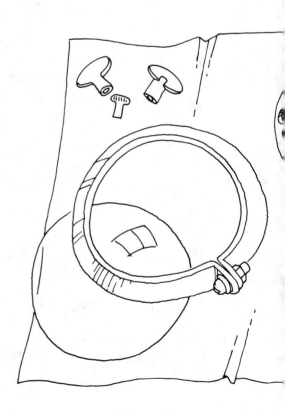

DECONSTRUCTION

1. Find a suitable place to perform the dissection. Remember that you may need the work area for several days, so plan accordingly (you won't want your partly disassembled contraption to be in anyone's way).

2. Cover the work surface with newspapers. Use rags to clean any grease or dirt off the device you plan to take apart.

3. Carefully examine the outside of the device. Try to imagine what may be inside. Then observe it carefully to find out what keeps the device from falling apart. Look for screws and bolts that fasten parts of the device together. If you are studying an electrical gadget, **be sure it is not plugged into an electrical outlet.**

4. Proceed to take the device apart. Make a list of each part and the order in which you removed it since you will want to put the machine back together again later. Use the form on page 76. (Teachers may reproduce the form for classroom use.) Another way to keep track of the parts is to place them in order of removal on a large sheet of drawing paper.

5. As you continue to dissect your device, try to figure out how each part relates to other parts. Try to understand how the machine works. Some of the references listed on page 72 may be helpful.

6. When you have completed the dissection, take a rest. Then put the device back together again! Refer to your list for help.

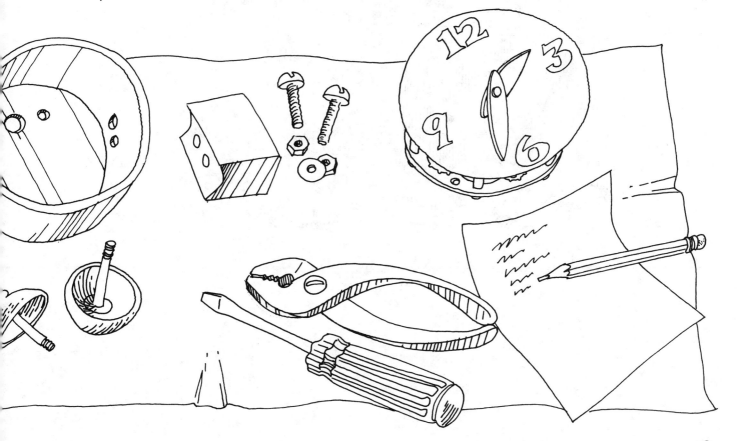

1. Take your device apart again, without keeping a list of the order of removal of parts. Throw all the parts together into a box and mix them up. Then try to put the machine back together!
2. Remove some working mechanisms from several different discarded gadgets. See if you can put these mechanisms together into an entirely new machine that will do some job.
3. Make a "Great Gadgets of the World Collection." Mount various types of junkyard jewels such as switches, gears, and valves on wooden or fiberboard display plaques. Label each part and write an explanation of how it works.

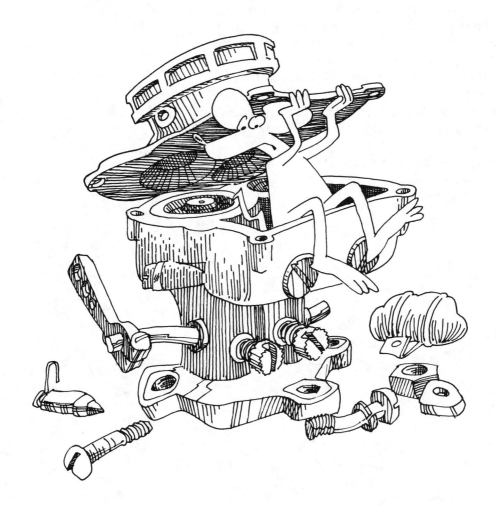

2

Inside-the-Box Inventions

Inside-the-box inventions inspire kids' curiosity about the internal mechanisms that make machines work. Success with these particular activities and projects will require visual thinking skills and careful work. After discovering the tricks to such mysterious contraptions as the Water-Expanding Machine and the Mysterious X-Ray Machine, some ambitious kids may want to invent an entire line of devices for a magic act.

Mysterious Pushrod Boxes

Did you ever look at an automatic pencil sharpener, candy vending machine, or other mechanical marvel and think, "I wonder how that thing works?" Figuring out how other inventors have built their devices is a good exercise in imagination.

Pushrod boxes are problems that require kids to use the same mental gymnastics. The three pushrod box problems presented here are repeated on activity sheets on pages 77–79. Teachers may reproduce these sheets for classroom use. Solutions to the problems are provided in Inventors Notes and Solutions on page 71.

Some kids have called these "Do-Nothing Boxes" because they are not designed to do anything useful (except stimulate some thinking!). The actual working models of the pushrod boxes were constructed from old cigar boxes and wooden dowels, and they have some hidden innards constructed from simple everyday materials. The arrangement of the innards connecting the visible wooden dowels determines the movements of these dowels. The pushrod box problems in this book, however, do not involve real construction, just some imagined construction.

MATERIALS

Pencil with eraser
Paper (or use the activity sheets on pages 77–79)

PROCEDURE

1. Study Pushrod Box Problem 1. Read through the operation carefully. Try to imagine what might be inside the box that connects rods A and B together.
2. Sketch your mental picture of the box's mechanical contents.
3. Repeat the procedure for Pushrod Box Problems 2 and 3.

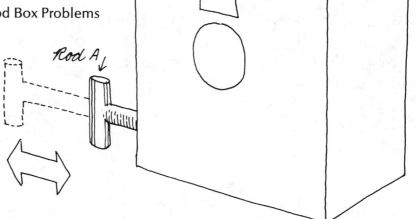

sealed old cigar box

wooden dowel with handle

Rod B

Rod A

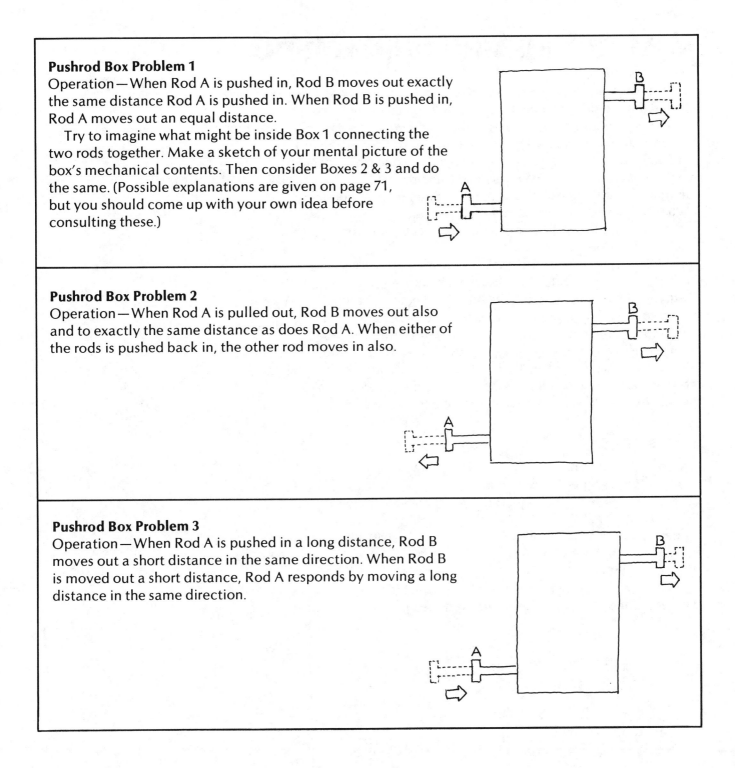

Pushrod Box Problem 1

Operation—When Rod A is pushed in, Rod B moves out exactly the same distance Rod A is pushed in. When Rod B is pushed in, Rod A moves out an equal distance.

Try to imagine what might be inside Box 1 connecting the two rods together. Make a sketch of your mental picture of the box's mechanical contents. Then consider Boxes 2 & 3 and do the same. (Possible explanations are given on page 71, but you should come up with your own idea before consulting these.)

Pushrod Box Problem 2

Operation—When Rod A is pulled out, Rod B moves out also and to exactly the same distance as does Rod A. When either of the rods is pushed back in, the other rod moves in also.

Pushrod Box Problem 3

Operation—When Rod A is pushed in a long distance, Rod B moves out a short distance in the same direction. When Rod B is moved out a short distance, Rod A responds by moving a long distance in the same direction.

■ **INVENTIVE SIDETRIPS**

1. With pasteboard cutouts and paper fasteners you can fashion actual working models of the pushrod boxes. Even better, build them out of old cigar boxes and dowels and see how good your friends are at figuring out how they work.

2. Invent an original mysterious pushrod box (one that operates differently from those described here). Then build it!

Water Expanding Machine

An inventor once claimed to have developed a miraculous new device that could somehow triple the volume of a sample of water by expanding it. The water-expanding machine was constructed from a cardboard box with a funnel inserted at the top and a plastic tube extending through a hole in one side. The inventor never allowed anyone to look inside the box, but he demonstrated to many people that when he poured 17 ounces (500 ml) of water into the funnel at the top of the box, a triple amount—51 ounces (1,500 ml)—emerged from the tube attached to the side of the box.

Many people were suspicious that the inventor was not actually expanding the water, but was playing a joke on them. Scientists were inclined to think the machine somehow added water to the amount poured through the funnel, but it took quite some time before it was determined how this might be done. The instructions that follow show how kids can build a Water-Expanding Machine that will puzzle and astound their friends. Before proceeding, however, kids might want to make a sketch explaining how they think the machine works.

MATERIALS

Sharp utility knife or scissors
Half-gallon (1.89 liter) milk carton
Cardboard box—any size larger than 12 inches x 8 inches x 4 inches (31 mm x 21 mm x 10 mm)
3 feet (90 cm) plastic or rubber tubing—3/8–1/2 inch (0.8–1.5 cm) inside diameter is good
Plastic or glass funnel
Pitcher or large jar to pour water into the machine
Larger jar or tin can to catch water from the machine

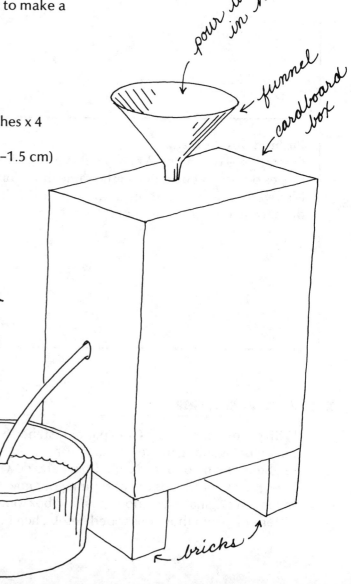

pour water in here

funnel

cardboard box

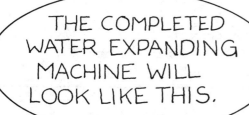

THE COMPLETED WATER EXPANDING MACHINE WILL LOOK LIKE THIS.

water runs into catch container

bricks

CONSTRUCTION

1. Start construction by using a knife to remove the peaked top of the milk carton.
2. Use your knife or scissors to make a round hole 1½ inches (3.5 cm) down from the top on one side of the milk carton. The hole should be of a size that the flexible tubing fits snugly in the hole, or it may leak.
3. Place the milk carton inside the cardboard box. Orient the hole toward the side of the cardboard box you wish the output tube for the expanded water to pass through. Punch a hole in the side of the cardboard box to match the hole in the milk container.
4. Thread a length of flexible tubing through both holes so the tubing just touches the milk container's base. The other end of the tubing should dangle outside the cardboard box and extend to a point below the base of the box.
5. Punch a hole in the top of the cardboard box directly above the open top of the milk carton. Place the end of the funnel in this opening. Attach a short piece of flexible tubing to the spout of the funnel (inside the cardboard box) and position this so it hangs inside the open milk carton.
6. Fill the milk carton with water to a point where the water level just reaches the level section of the output tube (as shown in the diagram of the Water-Expanding Machine). Place a catch container at the end of the output tube.
7. Now you are ready to operate your machine. Pour some water into the funnel. As the water level inside the milk carton rises, water soon begins running out of the output tube. This creates a siphon which doesn't stop flowing until all water in the milk carton has been drained away.

■ INVENTIVE SIDETRIPS

1. Modify the machine so it not only expands the volume of water put into it, but also apparently changes the water to some other liquid.
2. Invent your own illusion machine. Need some starter ideas? How about a machine that apparently dyes handkerchiefs? One that changes rocks to sand? One that changes a red ball to a white ball?

cut off top at this crease

hole 1½ inches from top side

MILK

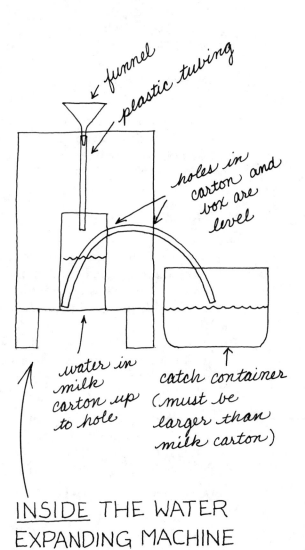

funnel

plastic tubing

holes in carton and box are level

water in milk carton up to hole

catch container (must be larger than milk carton)

INSIDE THE WATER EXPANDING MACHINE

Smoke Ring Machine

I'll never forget the huge advertising billboard that used to dominate Times Square in New York City. The billboard pictured a gigantic man smoking a cigarette. The thing I remember most is that real smoke rings were produced from an opening between the man's lips!

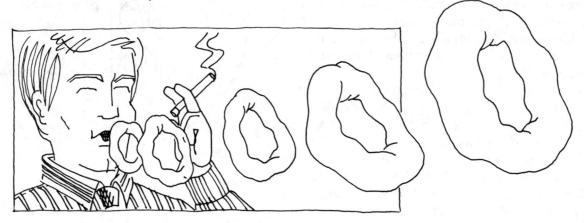

I wondered for a long time how the smoke rings could be produced, and finally designed a simple way to do the job. The resulting smoke ring machine is easy to build and fun to experiment with.

MATERIALS

Drill
Wooden box with 1 open side 5 inches (13 cm) square to 2 feet (60 cm) square (you can find or build one from plywood)
Aluminum foil or shallow metal tray
Piece of flexible plastic sheeting (slightly larger than one face of the box)
Tape (masking or plastic electrician's)
Brown paper bag, newspaper, rope, or commercially made smoke tablets
Matches

THE COMPLETED SMOKE RING MACHINE WILL LOOK LIKE THIS.

back has no wooden wall; this open side is covered with flexible plastic sheeting taped in place

paint face on wooden box →

hole in front

CONSTRUCTION

1. Drill a 2-inch (5-cm) hole in the center of the wall of the box opposite the open side.

2. Line the bottom of the box with several layers of aluminum foil (or place a metal tray on the bottom). This will act as a fireproof surface to hold burning materials for production of smoke.

3. Cut flexible plastic sheeting so that it covers the open end of the box and overlaps the sides by about 1 inch (2.5 cm). Tape the plastic in place along one side of the box. (Do not tape other sides until smoke-producing material has been placed inside.)

4. It is best to operate the Smoke Ring Machine out-of-doors or in a well-ventilated place (the smoke can be irritating in a closed room). To start producing smoke rings, use proper safety precautions to start a small piece of brown paper bag, newspaper, or rope burning on the fireproof surface inside your box. Don't let the burning material touch the sides of the box. Just after the material has flamed brightly, blow out the fire—leaving the material to smolder and make lots of smoke. (A good alternative is to use smoke-producing tablets available at novelty and magic shops.) As the material smolders, finish taping the plastic sheet so it forms an airtight cover on the open end of the box.

5. Allow the box to fill with smoke. Then tap or drum briskly on the plastic-covered side of the box. Smoke rings will emerge from the hole on the opposite side. When you are through operating your Smoke Ring Machine, be sure any burning materials *are completely extinguished.*

6. If you wish, you can paint a face on your box, placing the smoke ring hole between the lips of the face.

◼ INVENTIVE SIDETRIPS

1. What shapes of smoke puffs are formed if the hole of your machine is not round? Make pasteboard cutouts to fit over the hole to make a square, star, diamond or other kind of shape in the opening. See what happens when you operate the machine.

2. Will the Smoke Ring Machine work with dust rather than smoke? Place cornstarch or flour inside the box and shake it to create a dust cloud. Then try making dust rings instead of smoke rings.

Mysterious X-Ray Machine

Remember Superman's X-ray vision? With his super powers he could see through any solid obstacle, and observe anything hidden from view. Well, here's an invention that produces the illusion of vision through solid objects. It's not quite the genuine X-ray vision article, but it can provide almost as much fun. It can also provide a good scientific demonstration of mirror reflection of light.

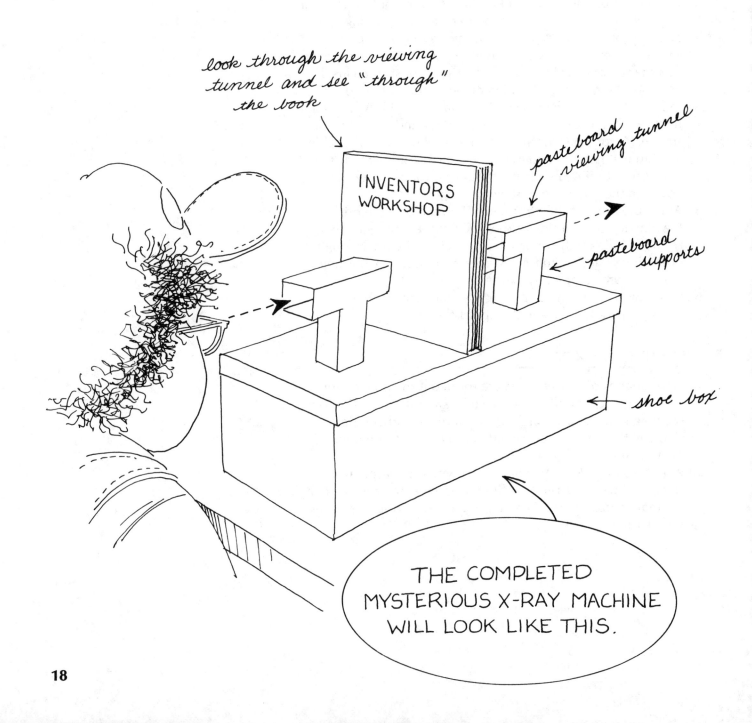

MATERIALS

Scissors
Poster board or stiff pasteboard
4 pocket mirrors
Protractor, if desired
Shoe box
Tape
Various objects to be looked through

CONSTRUCTION

If you place a brick, book, or any other solid object between the viewing tunnels of the box, you can apparently see right through the solid object. The mystery of how this works is explained in the following diagram:

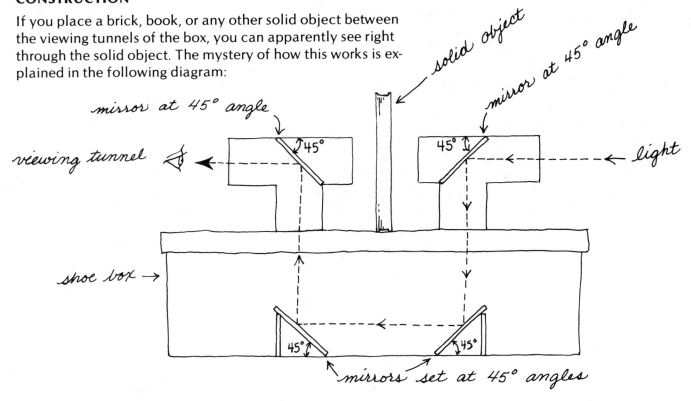

As you can see, the device enables you actually to see around a solid object, giving the illusion of seeing directly through it. This is accomplished by a precisely arranged set of mirrors.

1. Cut, fold, and tape together rectangular shapes of pasteboard to form viewing tunnels and their supports. The cross-sectional dimensions of the tunnels and supports should be the same size, and should be determined by the size of the small pocket mirrors you have on hand. A rectangular opening must be cut at the junction of each support and viewing tunnel, and mirrors taped in place at exactly 45° angles as shown above. (You might find a protractor useful for measuring the angles.)
2. Cut two rectangular holes in the top of a shoe box. Center one hole about 3 inches (8 cm) from one end of the top. Center the other hole a similar distance from the other end.

Use tape to fasten your viewing tunnel supports over these holes.

3. Position two mirrors at a 45° angle directly beneath the openings in the box top. (These mirrors should be placed about 3 inches or 8 cm from the ends of the box.) Fasten these mirrors in place with pieces of pasteboard and tape.

4. Look through the viewing tunnel and adjust all mirrors until the brightest view possible is achieved. Make sure all seams and joints are light tight.

5. Now you are ready. Place a solid object between the viewing tunnels—and look through it! Be sure to give your invention a good build up before having other people look through bricks, books, or even their own hands.

■ INVENTIVE SIDETRIPS

1. Figure out a way to give the illusion that you can see things inside solid objects (atoms or ghosts perhaps).

2. What illusion might be produced by placing a burning candle between the mirrors inside the shoe box? Try it and see. Be sure to take safety precautions so you don't set the shoe box on fire. Set the candle on a piece of foil in the box well away from the sides and top. Use a short, stubby candle.

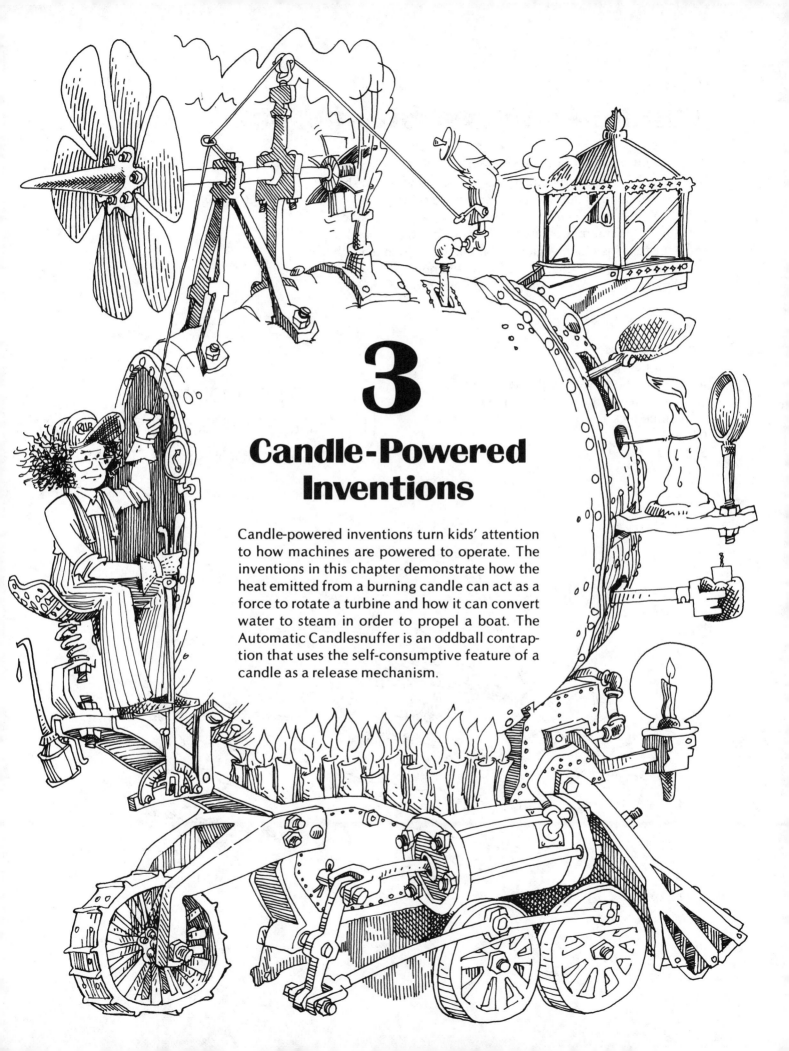

3

Candle-Powered Inventions

Candle-powered inventions turn kids' attention to how machines are powered to operate. The inventions in this chapter demonstrate how the heat emitted from a burning candle can act as a force to rotate a turbine and how it can convert water to steam in order to propel a boat. The Automatic Candlesnuffer is an oddball contraption that uses the self-consumptive feature of a candle as a release mechanism.

Candle-Powered Steamboat

The great steamships of the past century had complicated engines involving many moving gears, pistons, and metal shafts. But they depended upon a simple scientific principle: steam produced in a strong enclosure can develop a great deal of pressure. This steam pressure can be controlled and used to move pistons inside an engine. Or, it can be used in a much less complicated type of engine—a steam jet engine. This easy-to-build steamboat uses the simpler steam jet type of engine.

MATERIALS

Knife or scissors
Quart or half-gallon milk carton
Small oil can (the standard, old-fashioned
    type shown in the drawing below)
Nail or ice pick
Glue
Short candle
Matches

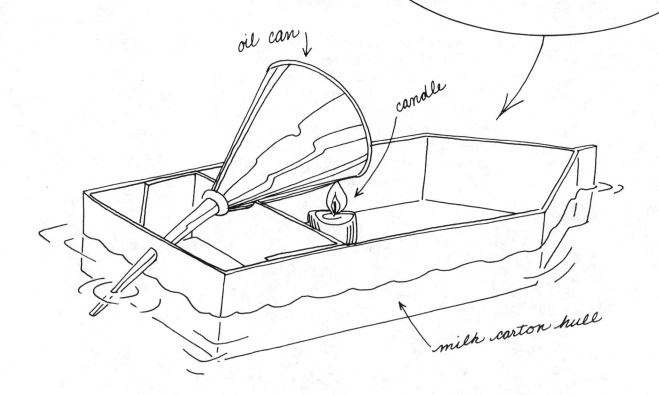

CONSTRUCTION

1. Slice the milk carton lengthwise about 2 inches (about 5 cm) from one side. (Measure from the back of the carton, the un-opened side.)

    Use the 2-inch (5-cm) side of the carton as the hull of your steamboat.

2. Cut about 2 inches (5 cm) from the bottom of the unused portion of the cut milk carton. Fit this piece in place near the stern of your steamboat to form a support for its oil can engine.

3. Cut a semicircular notch at the top of the engine support to accommodate the neck of the oil can.

4. Use a nail or ice pick to bore a small hole in the center of the lowest part of the stern of your boat.

5. Now, slowly force the stem of the oil can through this hole from the inside of the boat until about 1 inch (2.5 cm) of the stem protrudes through the stern.

6. Place and glue the engine support in place so that it firmly holds the oil can as shown.

    Place a candle under the oil can boiler, and you're ready to get under way!

7. A bathtub, pool, or pond would be a good place for the steamboat's maiden voyage. Half fill the oil can with water and position it in the boat. Place the boat on the water, light the candle, and be patient while the oil can boiler builds up a head of steam. Bon voyage!

■ INVENTIVE SIDETRIPS

1. Modify the heat source for your steamboat's engine or the engine itself to make the boat move faster.

2. Build another milk carton steamboat having its steam jet aimed parallel to the water at the stern of the boat.

    How does the speed of this boat compare with that of the original one?

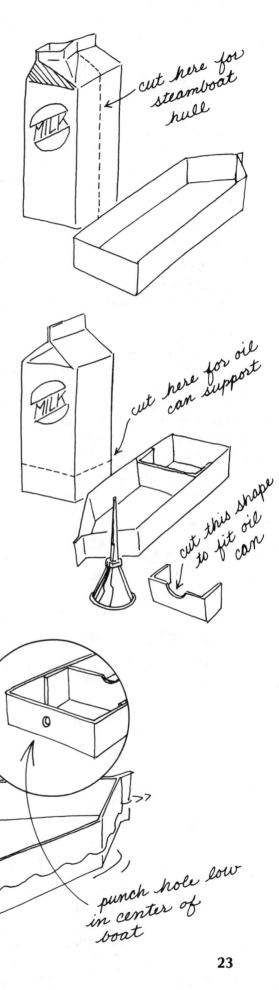

cut here for steamboat hull

cut here for oil can support

cut this shape to fit oil can

parallel to water

in the water

punch hole low in center of boat

23

Candle-Powered Steam Engine

Steam produced by boiling water in a rigid, closed container can develop a great amount of pressure. If steam under pressure is directed through a nozzle at a moveable wheel with vanes on it, you've got a steam turbine engine. Here's a nifty way to build one.

MATERIALS

Wire, wood, bricks, or tin cans to support oil can above the burning candle

Small pieces of aluminum from a pie pan 1 inch (2.5 cm) x 2.5 inches (6.5 cm)

6–8 inches (15–20 cm) stiff wire

Pencil or ball-point pen

3-inch (7.5-cm) square of heavy-duty aluminum foil or an aluminum pie pan

Scissors

Epoxy glue or clear plastic household cement

Oil can (the standard, old-fashioned type shown in the drawing below)

Candle

Matches

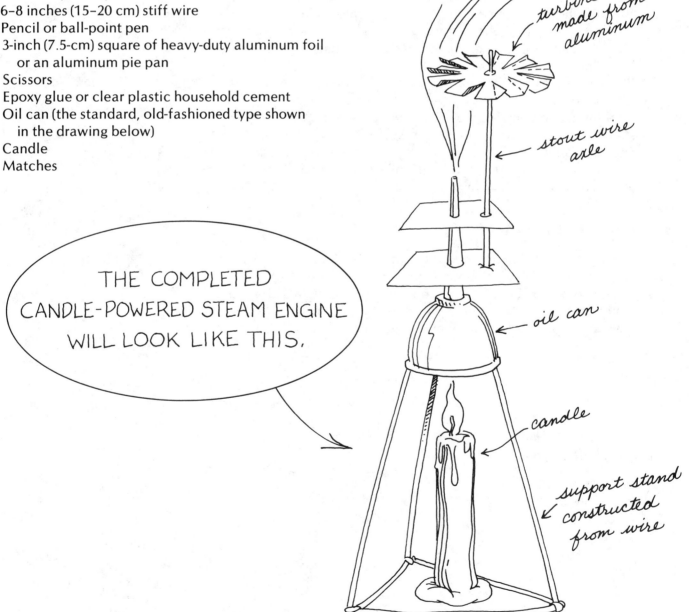

THE COMPLETED CANDLE-POWERED STEAM ENGINE WILL LOOK LIKE THIS.

turbine wheel made from aluminum

stout wire axle

oil can

candle

support stand constructed from wire

24

CONSTRUCTION

1. Use wire to build a stand to firmly support the oil can about 2 inches (5 cm) above the top of a candle. If you wish, two bricks or two tin cans may be used to support the oil can.
2. Cut 2 aluminum pie pan strips about 1 inch (2.5 cm) x 2.5 inches (6.5 cm) to use as turbine axle supports. Punch holes in each so that they can be pushed snugly on the neck of the oil can. Place one support 2-3 inches (5-8 cm) above the other, as shown.
3. Form an axle for the turbine wheel from a length of straight stiff wire. Punch a hole in the upper axle support about 1 inch (2.5 cm) from the oil can spout. Use a pencil or ball-point pen to make a small dimple on the upper surface of the lower axle support. This dimple should be placed directly below the hole in the upper axle support.

   Place the axle on the supports so the lower end rests in the dimple and the upper end is loosely held by the hole in the upper axle support, as shown. You should be able to turn the axle easily with little friction.
4. Use this pattern to fashion a turbine wheel. Copy the pattern on a piece of heavy-duty aluminum foil or aluminum pie pan and cut out the wheel with scissors.
5. Make cuts at all solid black lines shown. Fold up vanes on your wheel at dotted lines shown on the pattern.
6. Attach the turbine wheel to the upper end of the axle by pushing the axle through the center of the wheel. Use epoxy or other glue that sticks to metal to cement it firmly in place.
7. While the glue dries, add water to the oil can until it is about ⅔ full. Screw the spout firmly in place on the can and set up your engine on its stand above a burning candle. It will take 10 minutes or so to build up a head of steam, and then the jet of steam will cause the turbine wheel and its axle to rotate rapidly.

■ INVENTIVE SIDETRIPS

1. Find ways to make the steam turbine rotate faster. For example, try using two candles.
2. How powerful is the steam engine? See how many small paper clips can be pulled by a thread that winds itself around the rotating axle of the engine. Tie clips to 1 end of the string. Tie the other end to the axle, just below the turbine wheel. Add clips until they put a drag on the rotation of the axle.

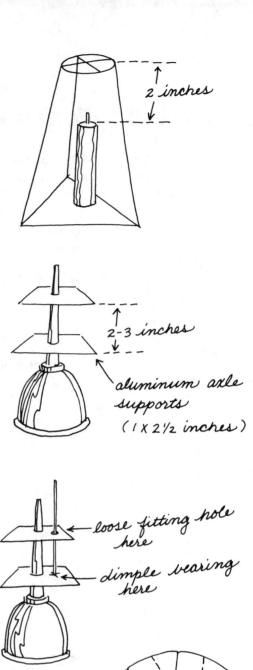

2 inches

2-3 inches

aluminum axle supports
(1 X 2½ inches)

loose fitting hole here

dimple bearing here

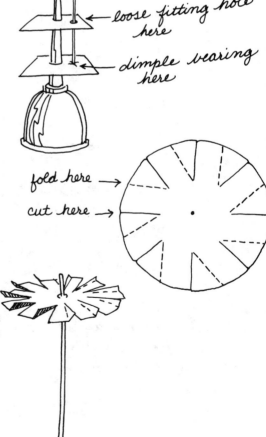

fold here →
cut here →

Automatic Candlesnuffer

Our great-grandparents probably faced one of the same problems we live with today—while reading, dozing off with the lights still on. The big difference is that our present day lights are electric while our great-grandparents' may have been candles or oil lamps. Admittedly, it's a bit late, but here is an invention that solves the earlier day problem of putting out a candle—automatically. Let's leave the problem of switching off an electric light for another day's invention.

MATERIALS

Half-gallon size milk carton
Candle in a weighted candleholder
Sand or rocks
3 nails
Old wooden spoon
Masking tape
String

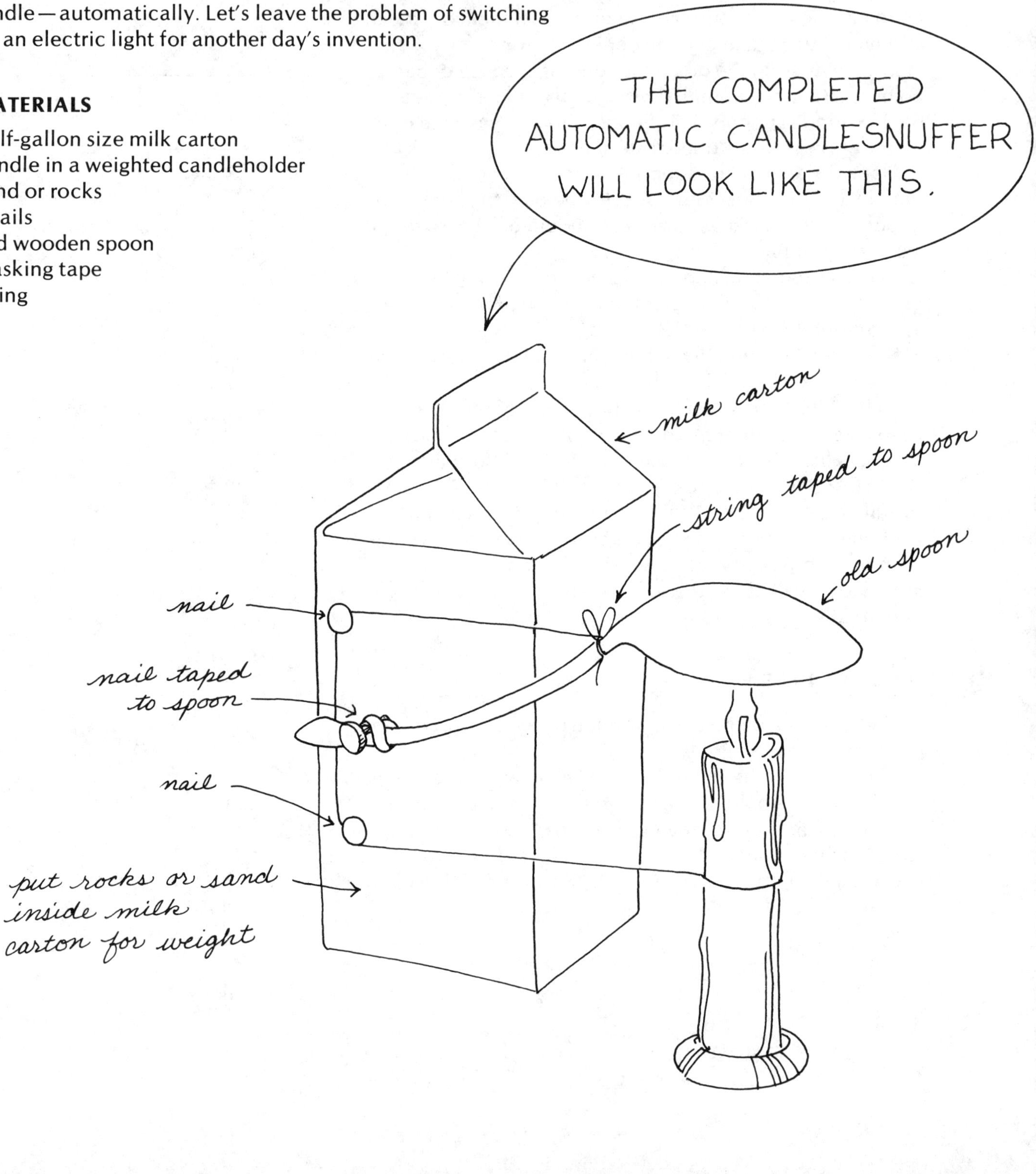

THE COMPLETED AUTOMATIC CANDLESNUFFER WILL LOOK LIKE THIS.

milk carton

string taped to spoon

old spoon

nail

nail taped to spoon

nail

put rocks or sand inside milk carton for weight

CONSTRUCTION

1. Stand the milk carton on a table next to the candle to be snuffed. Open the top of the milk carton so you can work inside of it with your hand. Place a 2–3-inch (5–8-cm) layer of sand or rocks at the bottom so that the carton is very stable as it stands on its base.
2. Stick a nail with a head on it through the wall of the carton from the inside at about the level of the top of the candle. The pointed end of the nail will protrude from the carton. Bind the end of the spoon to this nail with tape. (The bowl of the spoon should face downward.)
3. Position two other nails (heads outside the carton) as shown. Tape the ends of the nails inside the carton to make them stay rigidly in place.
4. Tie a loop in the end of the string and place this around the candle. The length of candle between the loop and the candle's top will determine the length of burning time before the candle is snuffed.
5. Thread the string around nail A, then nail B and then tape it to point C on the spoon. Adjust so the spoon is held about 3 inches (7.5 cm) above the top of the candle.
6. You're ready for a trial run. Light the candle and observe. When the candle burns down to the loop of string, the string is released and the spoon drops on the candle flame, extinguishing it. Voila!

■ INVENTIVE SIDETRIPS

1. Invent an entirely different method for automatically snuffing a candle.
2. Design a device capable of lighting a candle while no person is closer than 10 feet (3 meters) to the candle.

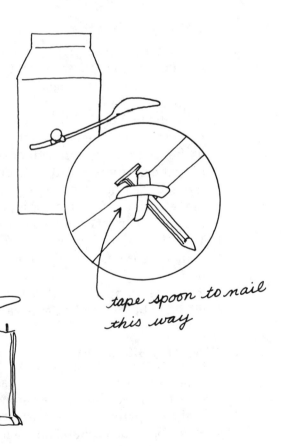

open top of milk carton

put rocks or sand in bottom of milk carton

tape spoon to nail this way

tape ends of nails inside milk carton

Candle Carousel

Most carnival carousels depend upon electric or gasoline engines to make them rotate. Here is a miniature carousel that carries its own source of power with it as it turns. The carousel floats on water and has two burning candles mounted on it. Bent aluminum foil sails are positioned above the candles so rising air currents produced by the flames push against the sails and rotate the carousel. Unfortunately, this type of carousel propulsion is not likely to put the larger carnival rides out of business: it is only powerful enough to move very lightweight devices. But it makes a delightful gadget to have some fun with.

MATERIALS

Aluminum foil
Scissors
Masking tape
Aluminum pie pan (8-inch or 20-cm diameter)
2 birthday candles (the thick type)
Sink or tub full of water

CONSTRUCTION

1. Cut two 12-inch x 3-inch (31-cm x 8-cm) strips of aluminum foil. Fold each of these in half to form a 6-inch x 3-inch (15.5-cm x 8-cm) rectangle. These will be the air current sails for your carousel.
2. Bend the two sails so that they curve over. Tape them securely to the inside bottom of the pie pan so that the curves of the sails face opposing directions.
3. Melt the bottoms of two thick birthday candles and stick them to the bottom of the pie pan with the melted wax. Place each candle so that it is positioned directly beneath the curved underside of each sail.
4. To make a more elaborate carousel, use horse-shaped aluminum foil cutouts and tape them along the edges of the pie pan.
5. Place the carousel so it floats on the surface of a tub of water, light the candles, and watch it rotate.

■ INVENTIVE SIDETRIPS

1. Experiment to try to make the carousel spin faster.
2. How much weight can the carousel rotate? Add paper clips to the pie pan to find the carousel's load-moving capacity.
3. How could the carousel be made to rotate in the opposite direction? Modify the carousel to test your ideas.

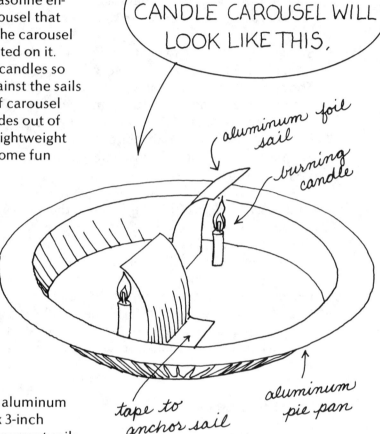

THE COMPLETED CANDLE CAROUSEL WILL LOOK LIKE THIS.

aluminum foil sail

burning candle

aluminum pie pan

tape to anchor sail

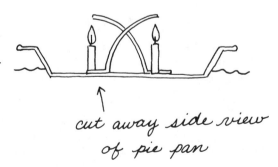

cut away side view of pie pan

4
Electrical Inventions

Electrical inventions allow kids to create simple circuitry and make a number of intriguing apparatus work. Two of the projects—Magtron the Magnetic Marvel and Magnetta the Magic Dancer—explore principles of magnetism.

Electrical Switch

An electrical switch is designed to connect or disconnect two electrical conductors, usually pieces of wire. When the conductors touch, electric current can flow and the circuit is said to be *closed*. When the conductors are separated, an air gap prevents the flow of electricity, and the circuit is *open*.

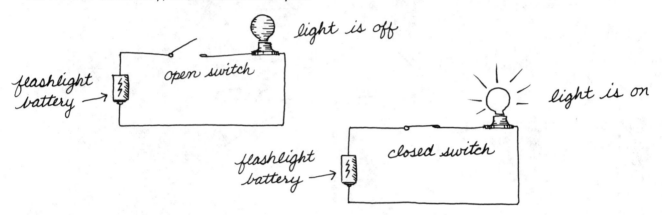

A simple switch is a useful gadget to have to control the operation of many devices that use electricity and electromagnetism. This project will provide instructions for making a good, usable switch from simple materials, and then challenge inventors to come up with original switching devices.

MATERIALS

Aluminum strip (5 inches x ¾ inch or 13 cm x 2 cm) cut from a
    disposable aluminum pie pan
Scissors or nail
Cardboard rectangle 5 inches x 3 inches (13 cm x 8 cm)
2 brass paper fasteners
Bell wire (about 1 yard or 1 meter in length)
2 flashlight batteries
Flashlight bulb with a bulb holder or a 3-volt buzzer (both are
    available from electrical supply shops or hardware stores)
Masking tape or electrician's tape

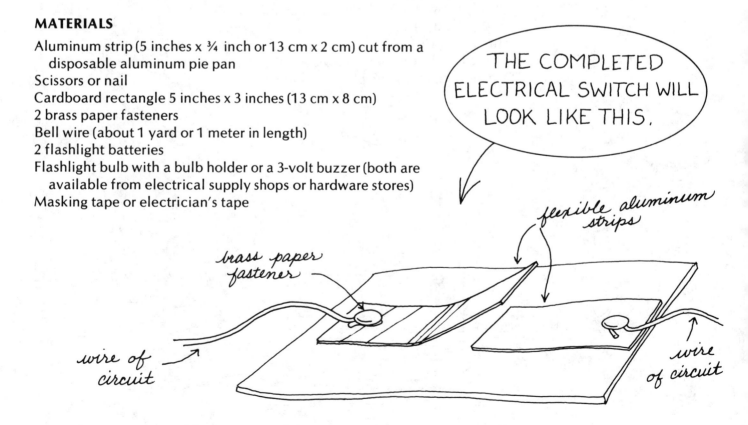

CONSTRUCTION

1. Cut the aluminum strip into two pieces—one 3 inches (8 cm) long, and the other 2 inches (5 cm) long.

2. Position the shorter aluminum strip on the cardboard base as shown in the diagram. Use scissors or a nail to punch a hole through the aluminum and the cardboard base. Push a brass paper fastener through this hole and spread the fastener's prongs open beneath the cardboard base.

3. Make a bend at the center of the 3-inch (8-cm) aluminum strip. Position this strip as shown in the diagram so the bent-up end of the strip overlaps the previously fastened aluminum strip by about ¾ inch (2 cm). Make a hole through the bent strip and the cardboard base, and fasten them together with a paper fastener inserted through these holes.

Note: If this switch is built properly, the two aluminum strips will not touch until you push the bent strip downwards. When pressure is released from the strip, it should spring upwards to its original position.

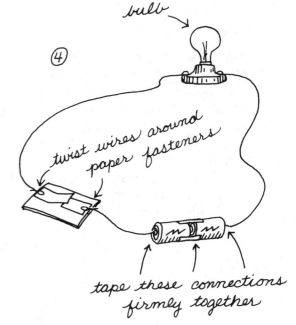

④ bulb

twist wires around paper fasteners

tape these connections firmly together

4. To give your switch a trial run, connect it into a circuit with wire, two flashlight batteries, and either a flashlight bulb or a 3-volt buzzer. Tape the tip-end of one battery to the flat base of the other, as shown in the diagram. Then firmly tape wire connections to the tip of the battery on one end and the base of the battery on the other end.

   The sequence used in taping the various connections makes no difference.

   If a commerical bulb holder is used, connect the wires to its terminals by wrapping the wires firmly around the screw terminals and tightening them with a screwdriver. When you press the switch, the light or buzzer should operate.

■ INVENTIVE SIDETRIPS

1. Now that you have the basic idea of how a switch operates, try to invent new types of switches from a variety of available junk materials. Here are some ideas:

   Invent a switch made from paper clips.
   Invent a switch made from a spring clothespin.
   Invent a switch made from a tin can.
   Invent a switch that uses a liquid to close the circuit.
   Invent a switch that opens a circuit when you press it.
   Invent a switch that closes a circuit when it rains.
   Invent a switch that could be tripped by an insect.

2. Use simple materials to build a holder for a flashlight bulb.

3. Invent a burglar alarm that would signal when a cat is prowling. (You will need to develop a switch that can be tripped by a cat.)

Steadiness Tester

We've all heard the saying "the hand is quicker than the eye," but is it also true that "the hand is steadier than the eye"? This Steadiness Tester will doubtless prove that most people cannot control fine motions of their hands as well as they think they can.

MATERIALS

Wire coat hanger or similar sturdy wire
Wire cutters, large pliers, or hacksaw
Sandpaper or emery cloth
Needle-nosed pliers
Thick cardboard (½–1-inch or 1.25–2.5-cm thick and 12 inches long x 6 inches wide or 30 cm x 15 cm)
Bell wire
Tape (filament strapping tape is good)
Flashlight battery
Flashlight bulb and bulb holder

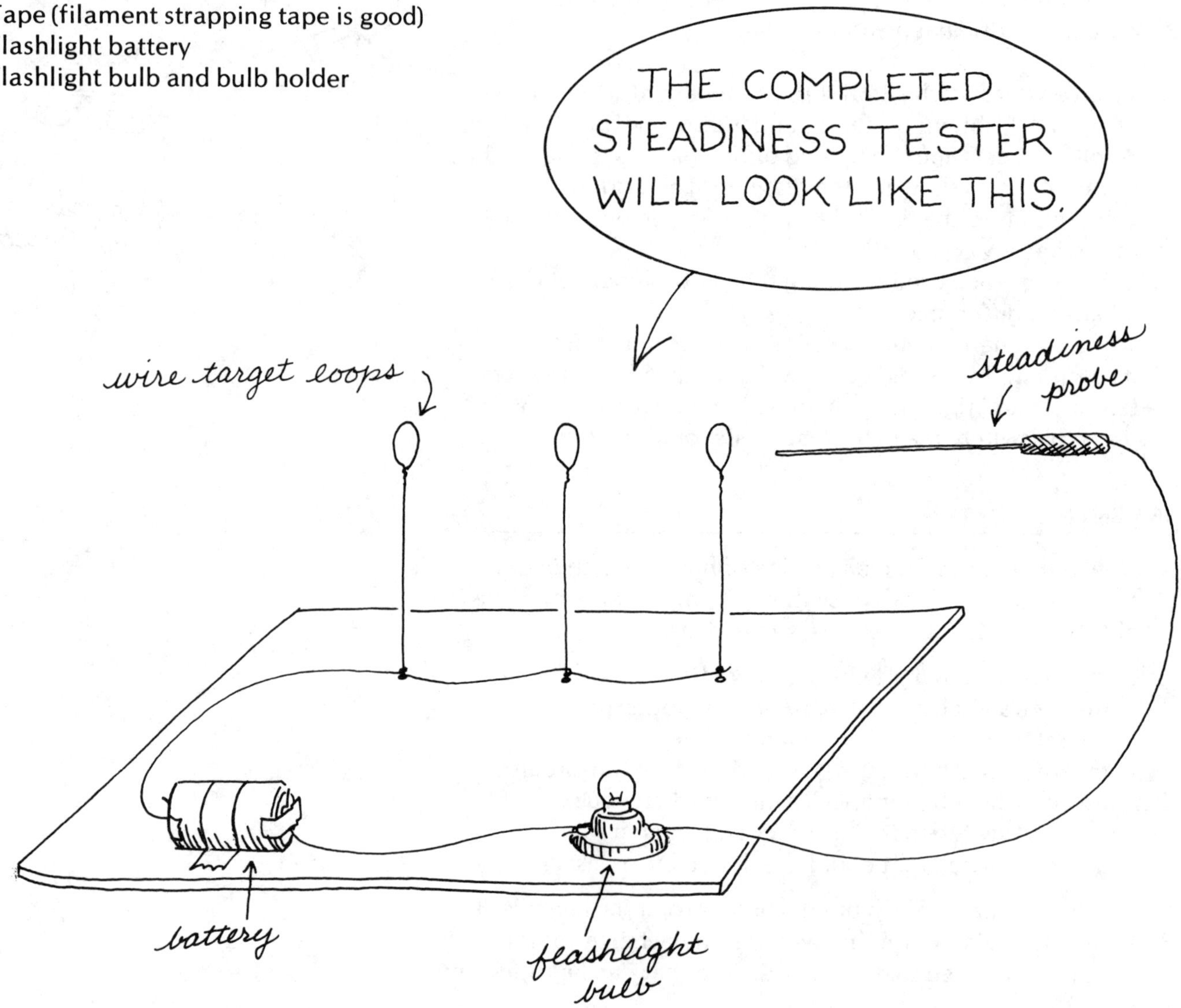

THE COMPLETED STEADINESS TESTER WILL LOOK LIKE THIS.

wire target loops

steadiness probe

battery

flashlight bulb

CONSTRUCTION

1. Cut three 8-inch (20-cm) lengths of coat hanger or other sturdy wire with wire cutters, large pliers, or a hacksaw.
2. If the wire is enamel-coated, use sandpaper or emery cloth to remove the coating completely from about 2 inches (5 cm) on both ends of each of the three pieces of wire.
3. Use pliers (needle-nosed type is ideal) to form a closed loop (about ¾ inch or 2 cm in diameter) at one end of each piece of wire.
4. Obtain a thick cardboard base and mark a 6-inch (16-cm) line about 2 inches (5 cm) from, and parallel to, one of the longer sides of the cardboard base. Divide the line into three equal segments.
5. Push the straight (unlooped) end of each of the pieces of coat hanger wire into the cardboard base so that they are equally spaced and standing upright along the line drawn on the base. Adjust the loops so their openings are perfectly aligned.
6. Run a length of bell wire along the bases of the loops to make an electrical pathway. Tape down the wire so that it touches each base. Connect this electrical pathway to one end of a flashlight battery with tape. Tape the flashlight battery to the cardboard base.
7. Tape another piece of bell wire to the other end of the flashlight battery. Wind the other end of the wire to one terminal of a flashlight bulb holder.
8. Make a steadiness probe from a 10-inch (25-cm) straight piece of coat hanger wire. Sand any coating off the entire surface of this wire, and then wrap the end of a length of bell wire tightly around 3 inches (7.5 cm) of one end of the stout wire. Cover up this junction by wrapping it with several layers of tape.
9. Attach the loose end of the probe's bell wire to the unused terminal of your light bulb holder. Now try out the device. Attempt to move the probe so that you penetrate all three of the upright wire loops without touching them. Whenever you waver enough for the probe to touch one of the loops, the light will turn on.

■ INVENTIVE SIDETRIPS

1. Devise a steadiness tester that activates a bell or buzzer instead of a light bulb.
2. Use the steadiness tester to do some scientific surveys of the relative steadiness of different groups of people. Are adults steadier than kids? Are women steadier than men?
3. Invent a steadiness tester that requires a person to move a wire loop along a curved wire pathway (instead of moving a probe through stationary wire loops).

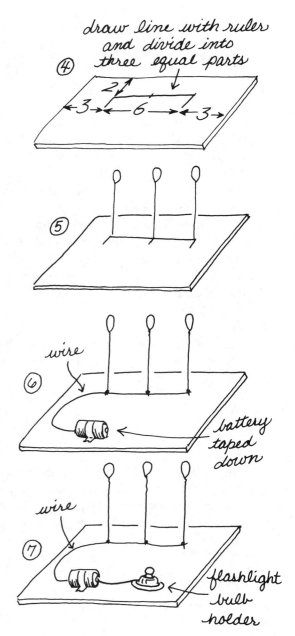

draw line with ruler and divide into three equal parts

④

⑤

⑥ wire   battery taped down

⑦ wire   flashlight bulb holder

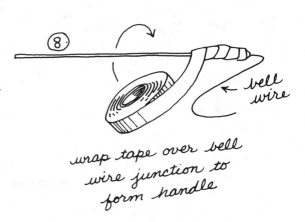

⑧   bell wire

wrap tape over bell wire junction to form handle

Magtron the Magnetic Marvel

Magtron is a kind of electromagnetic device that electrical engineers call a *solenoid*. Though the name sounds complicated, solenoids are really quite simple gadgets. They are usually constructed of a coil of wire wrapped in the shape of a tube. A moveable iron core is placed inside the coil of wire. When an electrical cell is connected to the wire, electrical current moves in a spiral path around the iron core. This electrical current has a magnetic field associated with it. The iron core becomes temporarily magnetic, and is repelled by the magnetic field of the coil of wire. Thus, whenever the current is switched on, the iron core is pushed out of the wire coil. Here is a drawing showing a simple circuit including a solenoid.

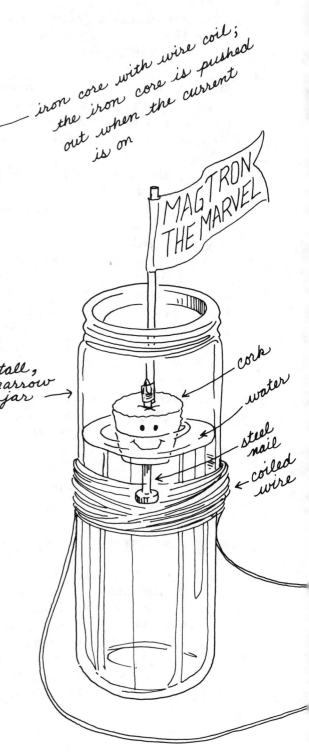

iron core with wire coil; the iron core is pushed out when the current is on

← flashlight battery

← doorbell switch

tall, narrow jar →

cork

water

steel nail

← coiled wire

Solenoids are widely used in automobiles and in household appliances to turn pumps and motors on and off.

Magtron the Magnetic Marvel is based on a novel variation of the solenoid principle; in this case, the moveable iron core floats in a tube of water.

MATERIALS

Steel nail (6 or 8 penny size)
Cork
Set of waterproof felt-tip markers or a
 set of enamel paints (the type used for
 building model cars and airplanes)
Scissors
Small piece of paper for a flag
Masking tape
Lollipop stick
Sandpaper or knife
Fine enamel-coated copper magnet coil wire (about 3 yards or 3
 meters of 28, 30, or 32-gauge wire)
Tall, narrow jar (such as an olive jar or an Alka Seltzer tablet
 jar) 4 inches (10 cm) or more in height and about 1½ inches
 (4 cm) in diameter
2 flashlight batteries
Simple electrical switch (instructions for making one are pro-
 vided in the Electrical Switch project on pages 30–31)

CONSTRUCTION

1. Push the nail through the cork. The point of the nail should enter the narrow end of the cork and stick out of the wide end. Draw a face on the cork with felt-tip markers or enamel paints, to give Magtron some personality.
2. Use scissors to cut out a small flag from paper. Attach this with masking tape to one end of a lollipop stick. Attach the flag with masking tape to the pointed end of the nail that protrudes from Magtron's head. At this point, Magtron will look like this:
3. Use sandpaper or a knife blade to scrape the insulating enamel off about 1 inch (2.5 cm) of each end of the enamel-coated wire. Wrap this wire around the tall, narrow jar to form a coil around the jar. Locate this coil at a point about one-fourth the distance from top to bottom of the jar. Be sure to have at least 75 turns of wire around the jar (the more turns, the stronger the magnetic force).
4. Set up flashlight batteries and a switch to form a complete circuit with the coil of wire wrapped around the jar (see Electrical Switch, pages 30–31).
5. Pour water into the jar to a level a little above the coil of wire. Place Magtron into the jar so he floats on the water.
6. Flip the switch to allow electrical current to move through the coil. Magtron will move down when the circuit is closed, and up when the circuit is broken. Try changing the direction of flashlight batteries in the circuit if Magtron doesn't dive up and down dramatically. (Also be sure all electrical connections are good and try different water levels in the jar to find the level that works best.)

■ INVENTIVE SIDETRIPS

1. Use the up and down movement of Magtron to accomplish some task.
2. Try to improve Magtron so that he bobs more dramatically.

paper flag

MAGTRON THE MARVEL

lollipop stick taped to pointed end of nail

face drawn on cork

head of nail

fine enameled copper wire

wires connected to batteries by masking tape

switch

flashlight batteries held together by masking tape

THE COMPLETED MAGNETIC MARVEL WILL LOOK LIKE THIS.

Magnetta the Magic Dancer

Magnetta is a paper and paper clip doll who prances up and down on a cigar box platform. This magical performance is caused by an electromagnet which is housed under her dance floor, and this magnetically attracts her steel paper clip legs. A switch turns the electromagnet on and off, so she dances up and down in response to surges of magnetic attraction.

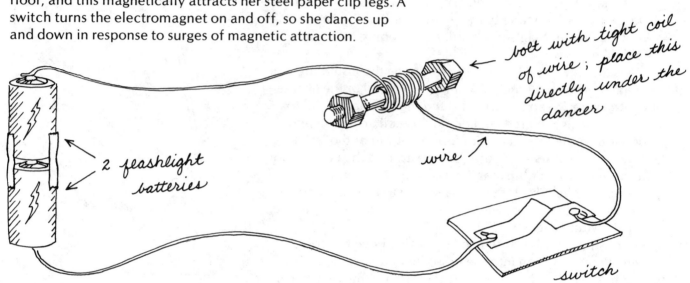

2 flashlight batteries

bolt with tight coil of wire; place this directly under the dancer

wire ↗

switch

An electromagnet is a simple device. You can build one by wrapping one hundred or more coils of fine enamel-coated wire around a steel bolt. Connect the wire in a circuit to two flashlight batteries and a switch. When the circuit is complete, electricity moving through the coil of wire creates a magnetic field around the bolt. While the electrical current flows, the wire coil and bolt electromagnet will attract iron or steel objects.

MATERIALS

Paper cutout of Magnetta's head and torso (you'll find an accurate scale drawing to trace on the activity sheet on page 82)
8 paper clips for Magnetta's arm and legs
Crayons, paints, or felt-tip markers
Pliers
Wire coat hanger
Cigar box or pasteboard box
Epoxy cement (or other cement that will bind metal to pasteboard) or staples
Fine enamel-coated copper magnet coil wire (3 or 4 yards or meters)
Large steel bolt, 1 to 2 inches long and ¼ to ¾ inches in diameter (2.5 to 5 cm long and .6 to 2 cm in diameter)
Sandpaper or knife
2 flashlight batteries
Electrical switch (see pages 30–31)
Rubber band

CONSTRUCTION

1. Draw and cut out Magnetta's body (head and torso). Attach pairs of linked paper clips to Magnetta's body to serve as arms and legs. Color Magnetta with crayons, paints, or felt-tip markers.
2. Use pliers to untwist a wire coat hanger to form a long stiff wire. Shape this as shown below to form a support for Magnetta. Obtain a cigar box (or similar box) and fasten this coat hanger support to one end with epoxy glue, staples, or with any other type of fastener you have available.
3. Construct an electromagnet. Do this by wrapping 100 or more turns of fine enamel-coated wire around a thick steel bolt. Sand or scrape the two ends of this wire so that good electrical connections can be made.
4. Cement the electromagnet inside the cigar box at a point directly beneath where the Magnetta puppet will dance.
5. Tape two flashlight batteries end to end inside the box. Tape one end of the wire from the electromagnet to the end of one battery. Connect the other end of the electromagnet wire to an electrical switch. Then connect the switch to the flashlight batteries.
6. Attach Magnetta with a single strand of thin rubber band to the coat hanger support. Position Magnetta so her paper clip legs dangle closer than 1 inch (2.5 cm) to the end of the electromagnet.
7. Make Magnetta dance: Close and open the switch repeatedly, switching the magnetism on and off. Magnetta will move merrily.

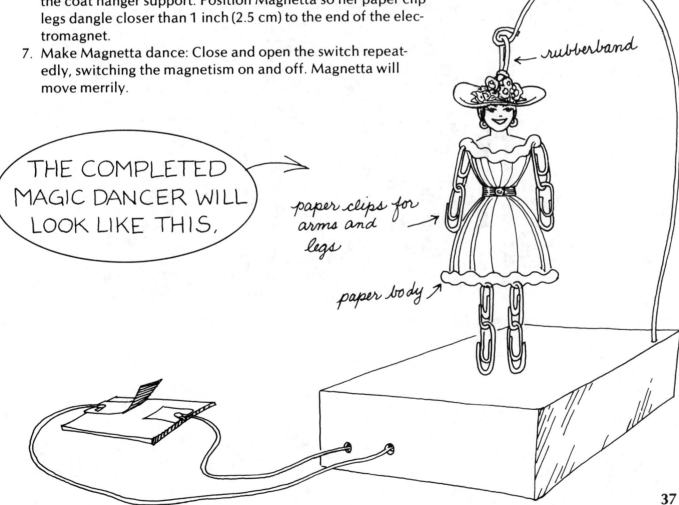

THE COMPLETED MAGIC DANCER WILL LOOK LIKE THIS.

wire coat hanger

rubberband

paper clips for arms and legs

paper body

1. Try to make Magnetta dance even more wildly. How high can you make Magnetta jump?
2. Now that you understand how to build an electromagnet, design a completely different device based on an electromagnet. Here are some ideas:

> Invent an electromagnetic paper dispensing machine.
> Invent an electromagnetic door opener for a doll house.
> Invent an electromagnetic bell ringer.

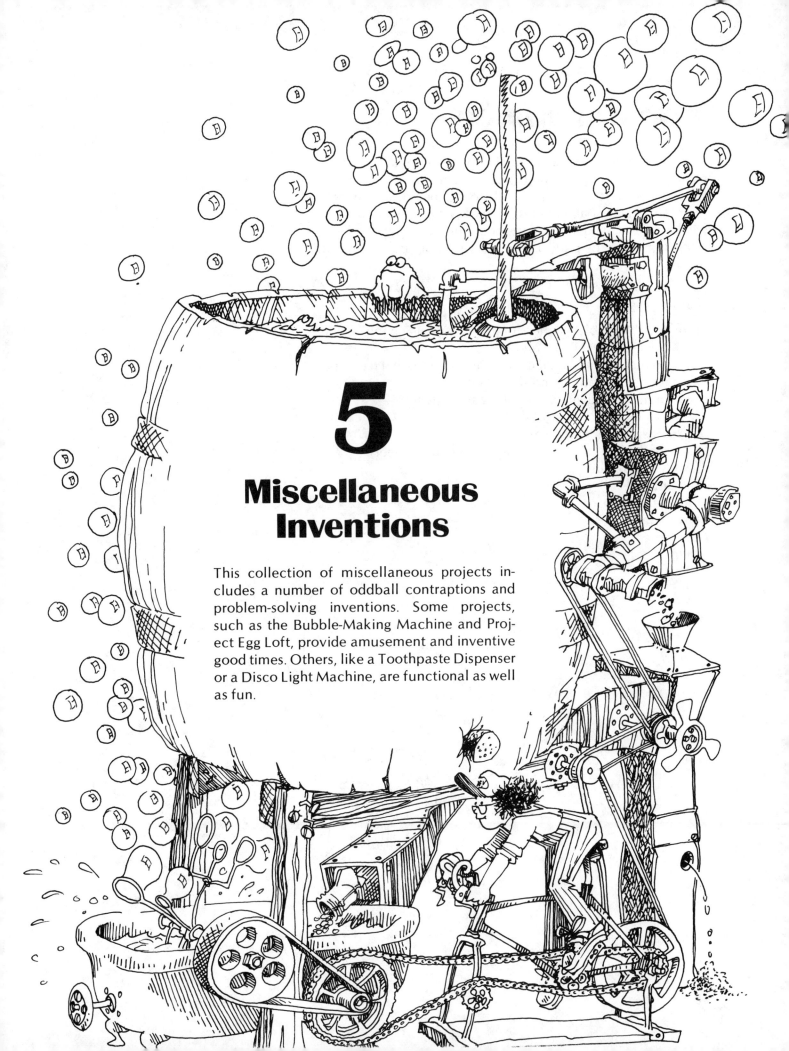

5

Miscellaneous Inventions

This collection of miscellaneous projects includes a number of oddball contraptions and problem-solving inventions. Some projects, such as the Bubble-Making Machine and Project Egg Loft, provide amusement and inventive good times. Others, like a Toothpaste Dispenser or a Disco Light Machine, are functional as well as fun.

Monster Bubbles

Almost everyone has made soap bubbles at one time or another
using plastic wands or bubble pipes obtained from a store.
However, all sorts of things found around the house may be
used to produce soap bubbles, and with a little ingenuity kids
will be able to make huge monster bubbles far larger and more
interesting than the puny ones made with store-bought bubble
makers.

MATERIALS

Store-bought bubble solution, or make some using this recipe:

  10 ounces (300 ml) of water
   3 ounces (85 ml) liquid dishwashing detergent (Lux brand
      is good but any brand should do)
  ½ ounce (15 ml) glycerine (also called glycerol—
      available at drugstores)
   2 teaspoons (8 ml) sugar

Large shallow flat tray (cafeteria tray or cookie sheet)
Flexible metal wire
Rubber bands
Drinking straws
Styrofoam cup
Coat hanger
String

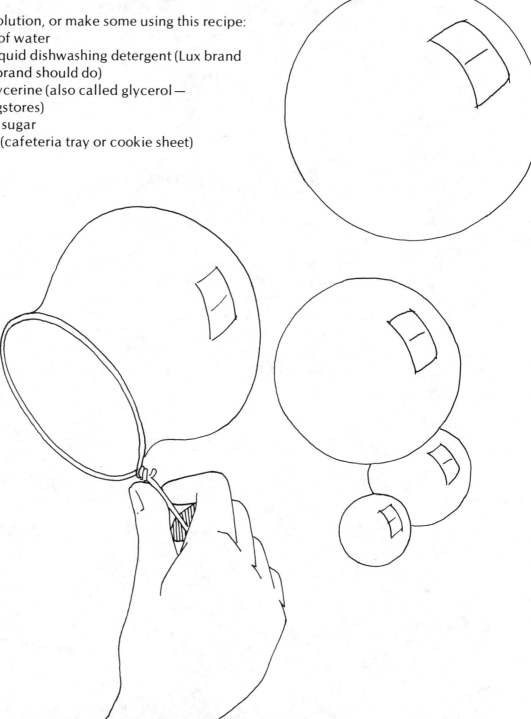

CONSTRUCTION

1. Obtain some commerically made bubble solution, or make some using the recipe in the Materials list.
2. Pour bubble solution into a large flat tray. Construct bubble-blowing devices like these:

blow gently here

← bubble wand made from wire

punch hole in styrofoam cup blow into this end

dip this end into bubble solution

drinking straw with end cut and spread open; dip this end into soap

← coat hanger bent into a circular loop

string supports soap film

drinking straw handles →

device made from 1 yard (or 1 meter) of string and 2 drinking straws

3. Dip the various devices in the bubble solution and blow on the bubble films (or wave the devices through the air). Try to develop the largest monster bubble you can.

■ INVENTIVE SIDETRIPS

1. Now that you have a start, see what other devices you can use for blowing bubbles. Try to use objects no one else would think of using.
2. Try to invent a way to make a bubble inside another bubble.
3. Can bubbles be made in different single colors (red, blue, green, and so on)? Experiment to find out.
4. Invent a way to make bubble sculptures.
5. Investigate dropping bubbles on different surfaces (cloth, wood, pieces of sample carpet, grass). See if you can find a surface that bubbles will bounce off of without breaking.

Bubble-Making Machine

Using lung power to blow one soap bubble at a time may be enjoyable, but think of the fun kids could have with a bubble-making machine that produces scads of bubbles quickly. Try this one for starters.

MATERIALS

Quart size milk carton (.94 liter)
Rubber cement or waterproof glue
Scissors or knife
9 inches (23 cm) stout wire (any metal will do)
Large cork (such as the type used in thermos bottles)
6 pieces of flexible wire (copper or steel) about 5 inches (13 cm) long (18–24 gauge wire is good)
4 brass paper fasteners
¾ quart (800 ml) soap bubble solution (see recipe in Monster Bubbles, page 40)
Electric fan or fireplace bellows

THE COMPLETED BUBBLE-MAKING MACHINE WILL LOOK LIKE THIS.

wire bubble wands stuck in cork

wire support for crank

brass paper fastener

stout wire crank

milk carton

CONSTRUCTION

1. Seal the spout of an empty milk carton shut with rubber cement or other waterproof glue.
2. Cut an opening approximately 1 inch x 6½ inch (2.5 cm x 16.5 cm) on the long side of the milk carton beneath the carton's pouring spout.
3. Make a crank and axle from the thick 9 inch (23 cm) piece of wire by bending it as shown:

make crank 2 inches (5 cm)

make axle 5 inches (12.5 cm)

2 inches

4. Force the axle through the center of the cork so it looks like this:

5. Bend small loops in both ends of two 5-inch (13-cm) pieces of flexible wire.

6. Bend the center of each of these two pieces of wire around the axle you previously made. Bend one piece of wire completely around the axle on one side of the cork and do the same with the other piece of wire on the other side of the cork. The combination of axle, cork, and two wires should now look like this:

7. The bent wires with looped ends attached to your axle will serve as supports for the axle to hold it above the opening you made earlier in a milk carton. Use brass paper fasteners pushed through the wire loops and into the sides of the milk carton to hold the axle and cork above the milk carton's opening.

8. Using 4 pieces of 5-inch (13-cm) flexible wire, make four bubble wands by bending a circle at one end of each wire. If the loops are about 1 inch (2.5 cm) in diameter, the wand handles will be about 2 inches (5 cm) long.

9. Insert the ends of the wire bubble wands into the cork so they are positioned like spokes in a wheel.

10. Pour bubble solution into the milk carton until the level of this liquid completely covers the bubble wand loops as they pass through the milk carton.

11. Place the Bubble-Making Machine in front of an electric fan or a fireplace bellows operated by another person. Turn the crank. With each full turn of the crank, four bubbles will be produced (one from each wand). Operate the machine out-of-doors if you don't want a room full of soap bubbles.

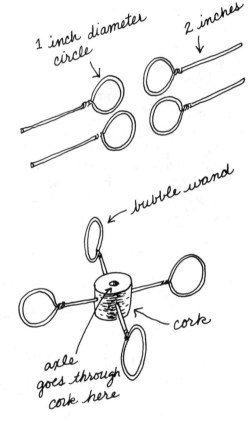

1 inch diameter circle

2 inches

bubble wand

cork

axle goes through cork here

■ INVENTIVE SIDETRIPS

1. Modify the Bubble-Making Machine to make larger bubbles.
2. Experiment with the bubble wands on the machine. What happens if they are much smaller? Bent into different shapes? Made from different materials?
3. Modify the machine to make zillions of tiny bubbles.
4. Invent a way to make the crank of the Bubble-Making Machine turn automatically.
5. Invent a new type of Bubble-Making Machine that is entirely different from the machine in this book.

Toothpaste Dispenser

A multitude of petty annoyances complicate lives around many households: somebody leaves soap in the sink, somebody else invariably forgets to tuck the shower curtain inside the tub, and everybody forgets to roll up the end of the toothpaste tube as they squeeze. Thus, the toothpaste tube in many homes becomes a rumpled and unsightly mess which certainly does not enhance a carefully decorated bathroom. Here's a nifty way to keep that bent up toothpaste tube hidden, while insuring that the paste is squeezed out evenly.

MATERIALS

New tube of toothpaste (complete with the box it comes in)
Cardboard or pasteboard
Scissors or knife
White glue
Straightedge
Paint (household enamel, spray enamel, or toy model enamel)
Short wooden dowel about ½-inch diameter x 1½ inches long or 1.5-cm diameter x 4 cm
2 round metal chair leg tips (the type that look like giant thumb tacks that can be hammered into the end of a wooden chair or table leg)
Small hammer

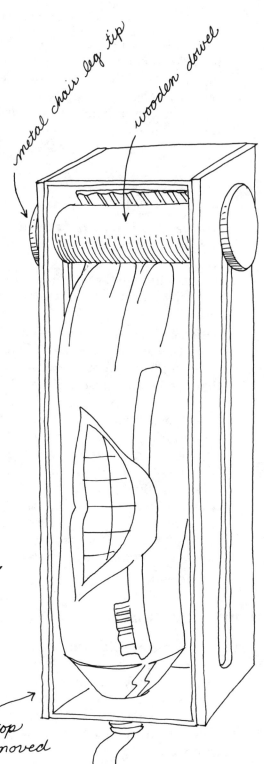

metal chair leg tip

wooden dowel

THE COMPLETED TOOTHPASTE DISPENSER WILL LOOK LIKE THIS.

view with top side of box removed

CONSTRUCTION

1. The toothpaste dispenser can be made from the box in which the toothpaste is packaged. Temporarily remove the tube from the box and cut cardboard strips to fit the two narrow, opposite sides of the box. Glue these strips firmly to the narrow sides of the box so that they reinforce these sides:

2. Bore a hole with a knife blade or scissors in one end of the toothpaste box to accommodate the uncapped nozzle of the toothpaste tube. It should fit tightly.

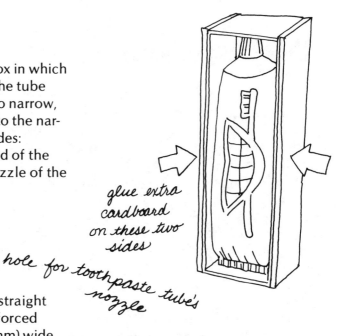

glue extra cardboard on these two sides

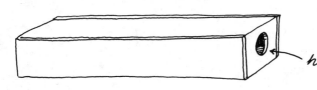

hole for toothpaste tube's nozzle

3. Use a knife and straightedge to carefully cut long straight slits on parallel lines drawn on the cardboard-reinforced face of the box. Make the slits about ⅛ inch (2–3 mm) wide.

make slits on each of the cardboard-reinforced sides

4. This would be a good time to paint the box. Allow the paint to dry thoroughly.

5. Make a roller to fit across the inside of the box from a short wooden dowel. Fasten the dowel between the slitted sides by hammering a metal chair leg tip into each end. (Turn the box on either side when you hammer in the chair leg tips.) Chair tips should be hammered into the dowel so it is held in place loosely—the dowel needs to be free to roll over the toothpaste tube.

6. Place the toothpaste tube into the box and you've got it— your own toothpaste dispenser. Turn the outside knob and press forward against the tube. This moves the roller inside the dispenser to squeeze out the paste. Be sure to replace the cap on the tube after removing the toothpaste!

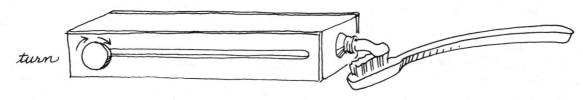

turn

■ INVENTIVE SIDETRIPS

1. Modify the toothpaste dispenser so that when you remove the cap it automatically squeezes out paste without anyone turning the roller.

2. Modify the toothpaste dispenser so that it doubles as a toothbrush holder.

Water Clock

For thousands of years, humans have been concerned with measuring small units of time. The first known clocks were sundials originated in Babylonia sometime before 2,000 B.C. Since these were dependent upon the sun, they were not useful at night or on cloudy days. So early inventors were concerned with designing other clocks that were not dependent upon sunlight.

One of the simplest and earliest timing devices (other than sundials) was a knotted rope. The rope was burned at one end and units of time were measured by the burning time between equally spaced knots. Hourglasses, using sand falling through a small opening separating two glass containers, were invented next.

Probably the most accurate type of ancient clock was the water clock. It worked by using drops of water falling from a small hole in the reservoir into a container. As shown in the drawing, as the water level rose in the container, a float caused a dial to gradually turn.

This project features a modern day version of the ancient water clock that is easier to construct but still produces a reliable Water Clock.

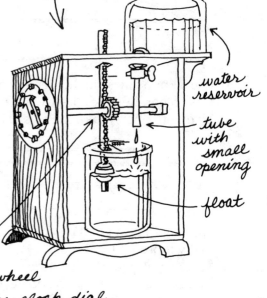

AN ANCIENT WATERCLOCK

water reservoir

tube with small opening

float

As the water level rises, this toothed wheel is turned, turning the clock dial.

THE COMPLETED WATER CLOCK WILL LOOK LIKE THIS.

MATERIALS

8–10 finish nails
Glue (for cementing wood)
Piece of wood for upright support about 20–24 inches (50–60 cm) long (an old broom handle or wood furring strip will do)
Piece of plywood or lumber for base (about 12 inches long x 8 inches wide x ½ inch thick, or larger [34 cm x 20 cm x 1.5 cm])
Piece of wood for upper cross support about 14 inches (35 cm) long (any sturdy but narrow strip will do)
Drill
Masking or plastic tape
Dowel or narrow wooden strip about 14 inches (35 cm) long for a moving balance beam
Plastic scoop (a measuring spoon or small flour scoop)
Wood screw
Several metal washers (large enough to fit around the wooden dowel)
Small cube of wood (about ¾ –1 inch on a side [2–2.5 cm])
Empty plastic cottage cheese container
String
Small bell, chime, or toy cymbal
Large tin can or similar container

CONSTRUCTION

1. Apply glue to the bottom of the wooden upright support. Position this at the center of the wooden base. Turn these upside down while holding them together. Then drive finish nails through the bottom of the base into the glued end of the wooden upright support.

2. Turn the now united base and wooden upright support over so they stand on the wooden base. Apply glue to the top end of the wooden upright support. Position the center of the wooden cross support on the top end of the upright support as shown. Attach the wooden cross support with finish nails to the end of the upright support.

3. Use a wood drill to make a hole through the center of a 14-inch (35-cm) wooden dowel or narrow strip. This piece of wood will be used as a moving balance beam for your clock.

   Use tape to attach a small plastic or metal scoop to one end of the beam and use a wood screw to attach several metal washers to the other end.

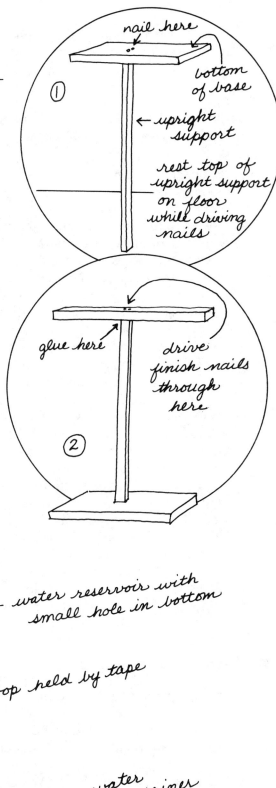

① nail here
bottom of base
← upright support
rest top of upright support on floor while driving nails

② glue here
drive finish nails through here

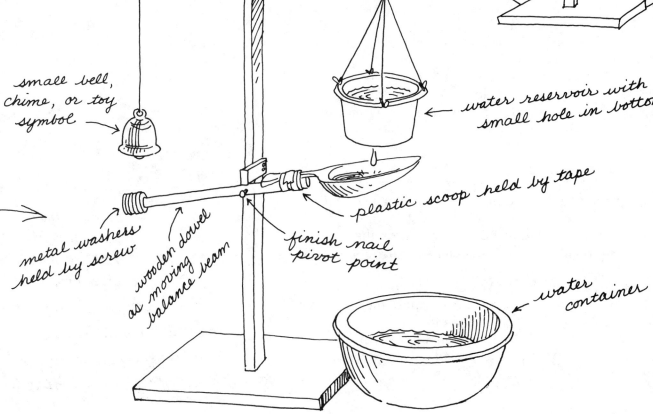

small bell, chime, or toy symbol

water reservoir with small hole in bottom

plastic scoop held by tape

metal washers held by screw

wooden dowel as moving balance beam

finish nail pivot point

water container

4. Use a finish nail placed in the hole drilled at the beam's mid-point to attach the beam to the wooden upright support a little below the center of the upright.

   The scoop and washers should be positioned as shown in the drawing, and the beam should pivot freely on the finish nail. Balance should be adjusted so the metal washers are a little heavier than the scoop (the scoop is balanced higher than the washers).

5. Nail or screw a small piece of wood on the scoop side of the wooden upright to act as a stop preventing the scoop from moving upwards too far.

6. Use a nail to punch a small water drop hole in the bottom of a plastic cottage cheese container. In the same way, punch three or four holes along the rim of this plastic container. Thread string through these holes and use the string to hang the container on the wooden cross support. Attach it so the water drop hole is lined up directly above the scoop.

7. Use string to attach a bell, chime, or toy cymbal above the metal washers on the other end of the balance beam.

8. Place a large tin can or other container below the plastic scoop to serve as a catch container.

9. You are now ready to operate your clock and make any necessary final adjustments. Fill the cottage cheese container with water. Water drops should drip into the plastic scoop, gradually increasing its weight. When the weight of the water in the scoop is sufficient, the scoop end of the balance beam should move down to the water catch container and pour its cargo of liquid into the container. At the same instant, the metal washers should clang against the dangling bell. This will repeat on a regular cycle, so you can use the intervals between the clangs as units of time.

   You may have to make adjustments in weight or in the positions of various parts of the clock. Once everything is finely tuned, the clock will work reliably as long as water is available in the cottage cheese container.

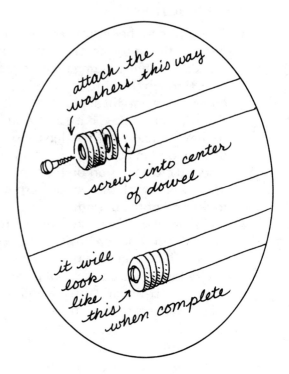

attach the washers this way

screw into center of dowel

it will look like this when complete

■ INVENTIVE SIDETRIPS

1. Use the completed Water Clock as a timer to time certain events—such as how long it takes an insect to walk a yard (or meter), the length of commercials on T.V., or the time it takes a shadow cast by a stick standing upright out-of-doors to move a measured distance.
2. Design improvements for the Water Clock. For example, rig up a flashlight battery and light bulb circuit to the clock that could cause the light to flash on and off.
3. Design and build a sand clock or a pendulum clock.
4. Obtain a discarded clock. Take it apart and try to figure out how it works.

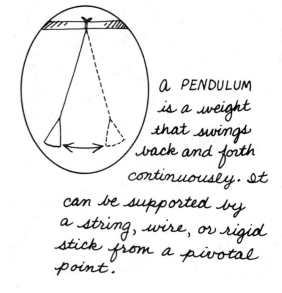

A PENDULUM is a weight that swings back and forth continuously. It can be supported by a string, wire, or rigid stick from a pivotal point.

Disco Light Show Machine

Discotheque dance parties depend upon two scientific ingredients—sound and light. The sound is usually recorded on plastic disks and played through loud stereo amplifiers. The dazzling psychedelic colored lights at discos are electric lights controlled by complicated electronic switch boards. Here are plans for a Disco Light Show Machine to use at dance parties.

MATERIALS

Jar or any other round object about 3 inches (8 cm) in diameter
10-inch (25-cm) diameter sturdy pasteboard circle
Scissors or utility knife
Transparent tape and masking tape
Colored cellophane (4 different colors, if possible)
White glue or household cement
Wooden dowel about 10–12 inches (25–30 cm) long
Aluminum foil
Flashlight
Cardboard box—any size larger than 10 inches (25 cm) tall and
    6 inches (15 cm) deep will do (a shoe box is fine)
Wire about 10 inches (25 cm) long cut from a coat hanger
Flexible wire about 12–14 inches (30–35 cm) long
Black paint (optional)

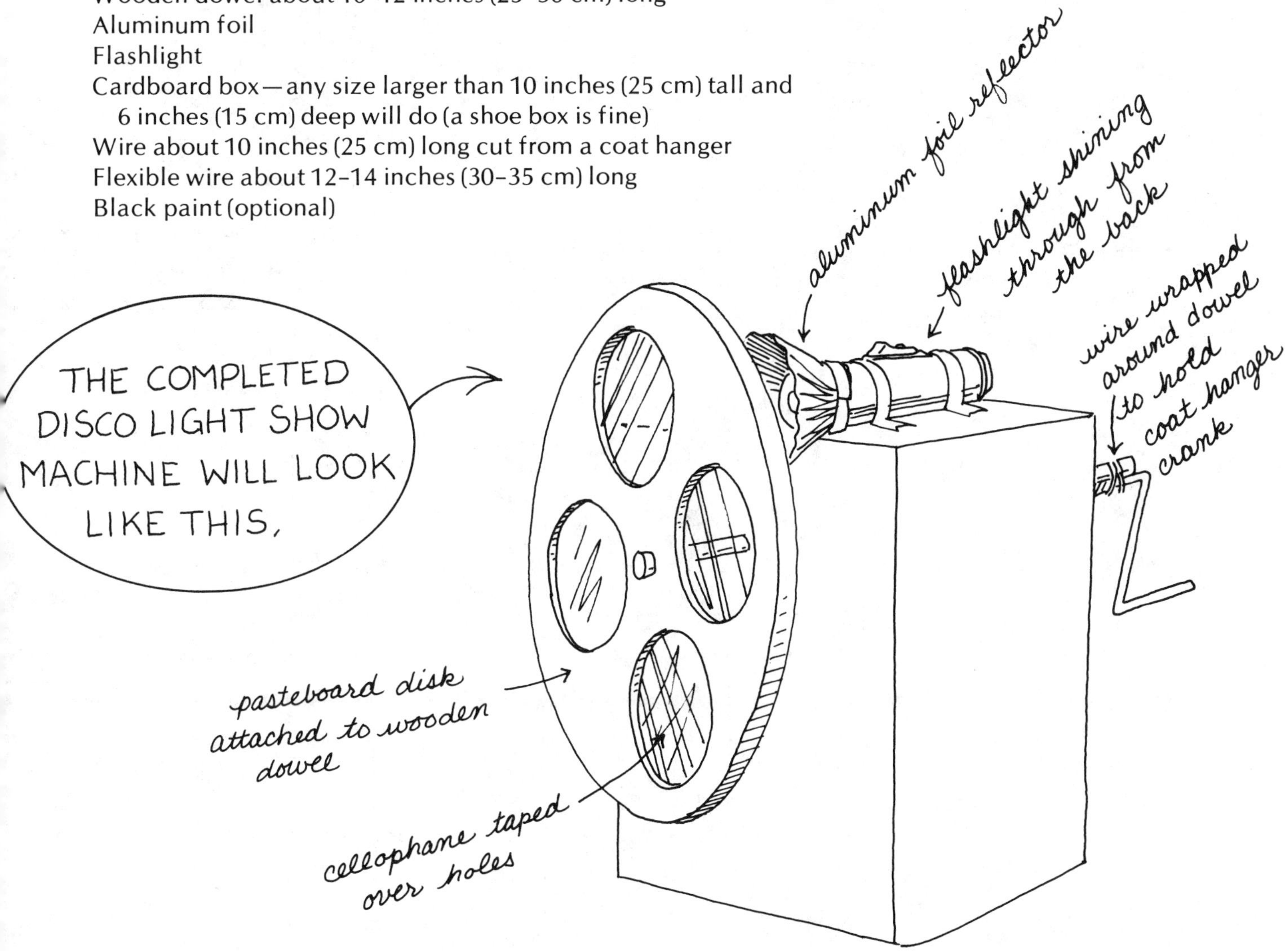

THE COMPLETED DISCO LIGHT SHOW MACHINE WILL LOOK LIKE THIS,

aluminum foil reflector

flashlight shining through from the back

wire wrapped around dowel to hold coat hanger crank

pasteboard disk attached to wooden dowel

cellophane taped over holes

CONSTRUCTION

1. Use the bottom of a jar or any other round object to draw four circles (about 3 inches or 8 cm in diameter) spaced as shown on the large pasteboard circle.
   Then use scissors or a utility knife to cut out the four circles, leaving four openings in the large pasteboard circle.
2. Use transparent tape to cover each of the four circular openings with a different color of cellophane.
3. Glue or cement the end of a wooden dowel to the center of the large pasteboard circle.
   Put this unit aside to dry.
4. Obtain a suitable cardboard box. Use scissors to punch holes in the centers of opposite sides of the box about 2 inches (5 cm) down from the top edges of the box.
5. Use aluminum foil and masking tape to construct a reflector (like a camera's lens hood) around the lens of a flashlight.

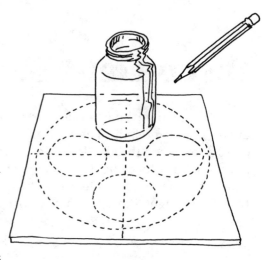

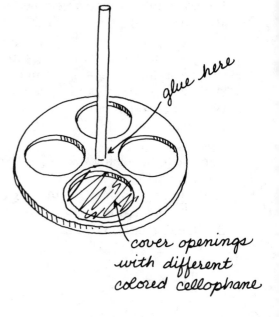

glue here

cover openings
with different
colored cellophane

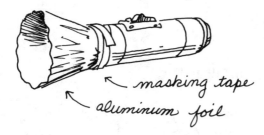

masking tape
aluminum foil

6. Use masking tape to fasten the flashlight on top of the cardboard box so the ends of the flashlight are positioned above the holes you punched in the box. The flashlight's reflector should extend over the top edge of the box about 1–2 inches (2.5–5 cm) as shown:

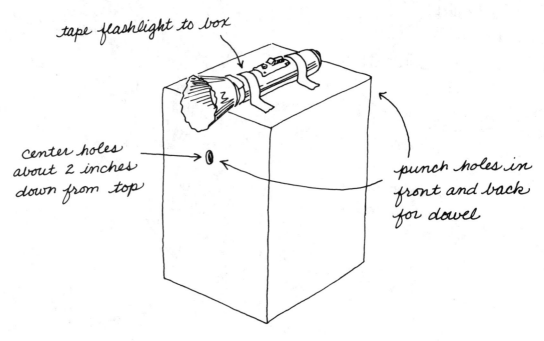

tape flashlight to box

center holes
about 2 inches
down from top

punch holes in
front and back
for dowel

7. When the glue has set on the pasteboard disk/wooden dowel unit, push the dowel through the holes in the cardboard box so that the pasteboard circle is held in front of the flashlight. Make a crank handle by bending a piece of coat hanger wire into a shape like this:

Use flexible wire to fasten this crank securely to the end of the wooden dowel that sticks out of the hole in the back of the cardboard box.

8. Paint the Light Show Machine black, or some other appropriate color.

9. To operate the Light Show Machine, take it to a darkened room. Play some appropriate recorded music, switch on the flashlight, and turn the crank. A sequence of differently colored light beams will be produced.

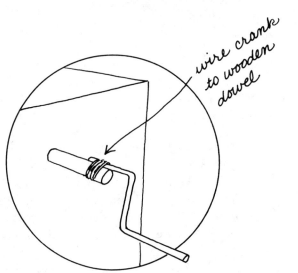

wire crank to wooden dowel

■ INVENTIVE SIDETRIPS

1. Improve the Disco Light Show Machine so it turns automatically. Be inventive—improvise some sort of motor to do the job.

2. Modify the Disco Light Show Machine so it produces sounds, as well as light, as it is cranked.

Operation Egg Drop

Humpty Dumpty sat on a wall,
Some sixth graders helped him fall,
All the king's men rode away in disgust
Because Humpty Dumpty didn't bust!

Cynthia Wong (age 12)

All the king's horses and all the king's men would be out of a job around some schools these days. Humpty Dumpty and his kin—dozens of them—have taken to leaping off tall buildings at a single bound, encouraged and aided by kids. But the king's omelet brigade isn't needed to clean up because very few of these oval morsels break, thanks to some cleverly designed containers.

Operation Egg Drop is an exercise in invention that has lately been used as a challenge to the imagination of both kids in grades four through eight and students in colleges of engineering. The challenge is this:

> Invent a package for a raw egg so it can be dropped without breaking from the roof or upper-story window of a tall building. You can package the egg in any way you wish, or attach things to it to slow its descent. However, you can't simply lower the egg on a string or a long stick—it must free-fall to the ground.

If you give the egg drop challenge some serious thought, you may be able to imagine all sorts of shock-absorbing packages and air-drag devices useful for assisting one of your local eggs on a trip from a high launching platform back to terra firma. Try building your own original solution to the challenge. Or, if you wish, follow the instructions for a super egg package as a starter.

THE COMPLETED SUPER EGG PACKAGE WILL LOOK LIKE THIS.

nylon stockings support egg in center of box

hole in side of box with knotted stocking

52

MATERIALS

Raw egg
Pair of old nylon stockings or pantyhose
Scissors or knife
Cardboard box (any size)
Paint, construction paper, or felt-tip markers for
   decorating the super egg package (optional)

CONSTRUCTION

1. Place a raw egg inside a nylon stocking (or one leg cut
   from a pair of pantyhose).
2. Wrap the center of another nylon stocking (or pantyhose leg)
   around the egg and the first nylon stocking and tie in a knot.
   If done properly, the egg will be held firmly at the midpoint
   of both stockings.

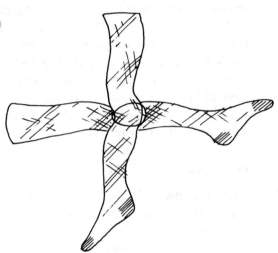

3. Use scissors or a knife to bore holes in the centers of four
   sides of a cardboard box. Decorate the box with paint, construction paper, or felt-tip markers.
4. Place each loose end of the nylon stockings through a hole
   in the box, threading from inside to outside. Pull the stockings until they are taut and make a large knot in each stocking. The egg should be supported by the stockings at about
   the center of the inside of the box.
5. Drop the box from any height. When this super egg package
   is dropped, the flexible stockings absorb the shock of impact, and it is nearly impossible for the egg to break.

■ INVENTIVE SIDETRIPS

1. Invent a super egg package that uses marshmallows as
   shock absorbers.
2. Devise a way to prevent a dropped egg from breaking using
   only balloons and string.
3. Invent an air-drag device you can attach to a packaged egg
   to slow down its speed when dropped.
4. Invent a super egg package that purposely collapses on impact to absorb shock.
5. Develop a motorized super egg package.

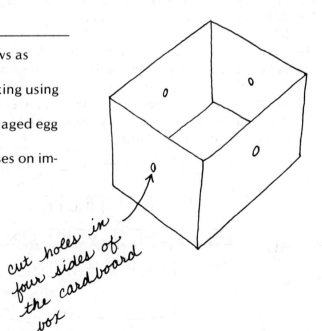

cut holes in
four sides of
the cardboard
box

Project Egg Loft

Project Egg Loft is an off-shoot of Operation Egg Drop. It is also characterized by flying eggs (some of which are suitable for omelets when they land). Like Egg Drop, Egg Loft requires the invention of a protective device to prevent breakage when an egg is dropped from some specified height. But, to make the problem more intriguing, you must invent a method or device to first lift the egg high above the ground, and then drop it. The method employed for lifting the egg should be able to operate independently of the direct use of human muscle power.

As you might guess, the Egg Loft challenge is not easy. A reasonable minimum height to be expected for the Loft is about five yards (or five meters), though kids have found ways to make an egg package fly much higher. The plans for one successful Egg Loft invention (which was designed by a pair of 12-year-old boys) are below. After you build it, design your own solution to the challenge.

MATERIALS

Small styrofoam box 4–8 inches (10–20 cm) on a side (these are used to package new clocks and other items)
Raw egg
Foam rubber padding (or other shock-absorbing material)
String (20 or more yards or meters long)
Handkerchief or other cloth or plastic for a small parachute
Flexible wire—about 8 inches (20 cm)
4 or 5 large rubber balloons
Helium gas (Helium may be obtained at welding shops, government weather stations, universities, some high schools, bottled gas distributors, or stores that sell helium-inflated balloons. If you scrounge around, you will likely be able to get some without cost if you say the material is being used for scientific experimentation.)

THE COMPLETED EGG LOFT INVENTION WILL LOOK LIKE THIS.

large helium-filled balloons

release device is two wire loops held by a pin

small parachute

small styrofoam box; egg is inside encased in foam rubber padding

string connected to release pin (pin is pulled out by person standing on the ground)

CONSTRUCTION

1. Obtain or build a small styrofoam box. (You can build a small box by gluing small squares of styrofoam together with white glue.) Wrap a raw egg in foam rubber padding (or other shock-absorbing material) and seal it inside the box.

2. Make the parachute by tying string to the corners of a handkerchief or other square piece of cloth or a plastic sheet. Attach the parachute to the egg-containing styrofoam box. To accomplish this, make two small holes near the center of the top of the box, loop string through these holes, and tie this string to the knot that holds together the four strings of the parachute.

3. Attach a short (12-inch or 30-cm) piece of string to the center of the parachute by either tying it to a small bit of material gathered at the center of the top of the parachute, or by sewing it on with a needle and thread.

4. Use wire to make a short pin (about 1 inch or 2.5 cm long) with a loop on one end.

Use two other pieces of wire to make figure-eight shaped loops that fit just snugly on the pin as shown.

figure-eight loops

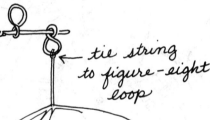

tie string to figure-eight loop

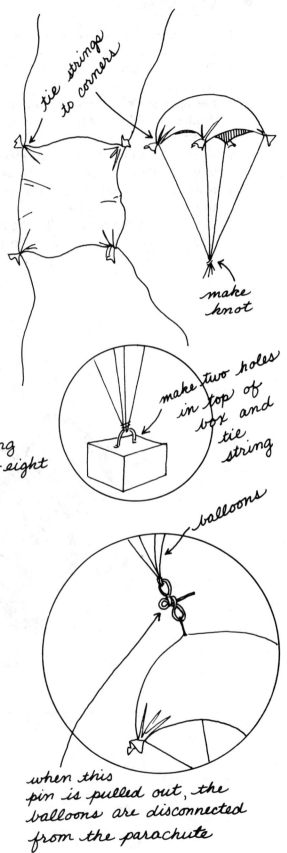

tie strings to corners

make knot

make two holes in top of box and tie string

balloons

when this pin is pulled out, the balloons are disconnected from the parachute

5. Tie the string attached to the parachute's top to one of the figure-eight loops.

6. Fill four or five large balloons with helium. Attach a string to each balloon, and tie the loose ends of the strings together in a knot. Attach this knot to the second figure-eight wire loop you fitted earlier to your wire pin. When finished, the release mechanism for parachuting your egg container will look like the drawing at the right.

7. Tie the end of a long string (at least 10 yards or meters) to the wire loop on your release mechanism's pin.

8. Now it's launch time. Allow the helium balloons to lift the contraption skyward. Pull the string on the release pin. This will separate the parachute carrying the egg from the balloons. If all goes well, the egg will be deposited gently on the ground by the parachute. You can either let the balloons go or have another string attached to them so you can retrieve them.

1. Use helium balloons to loft another egg, but design an entirely different container for carrying the egg.
2. Design and build a catapult to loft an egg package.
3. Build an egg-carrying kite.
4. Design a spring or rubber band device to loft an egg. Thick circles of rubber cut from inner tubes make powerful rubber bands.
5. Modify a commercially made model rocket to carry an egg upwards. (Note safety instructions accompanying rocket.)
6. Have an Egg Loft contest. Offer prizes for the Egg Loft contraption that: a) flies the highest; b) is the most complicated; c) is the best engineered; d) is the most artistically attractive; and, e) is the most unusual or most creative.

6
Product Test Inventions

Manufacturers make grand claims for their products: one brand of glue is stronger than all the others; one brand of paper towels is the most durable you can buy at any price. How accurate are these advertised claims? How often has a "Number One Brand" turned out to be a real dud? Kids can test the qualities of various brands of household products by obtaining two or more different brands of the same product, deciding which features of the products to compare, and designing some scientific testing apparatus and procedures. Similar tests may be designed for noncommercial items or substances to discover more about their properties. In this chapter, kids can begin constructing equipment for testing paper towel durability and egg strength.

Paper Towel Tester

Here is a simple procedure for running quality tests on different brands of paper towels. Once you have set up a simple apparatus, compare these characteristics of the towels: wet strength, water absorbency, scrubbing durability, and softness. Consider the cost per towel for each brand and the test results in deciding which brand is the best buy.

MATERIALS

Scissors
2 or more brands of paper towels
Yard or meter stick
Masking tape
Cardboard boxes, stacks of books, or other supports
Spring-type paper clasp
Flexible wire
Set of equal weights (washers, paper clips, steel nails—any large collection of objects having uniform weight)
2 or more glasses filled with water
String (1 yard or 1 meter in length)
2 paper cups (coffee or soft drink cups)
Ruler
Balance scale
Several paper bags

PROCEDURE

1. To test dry strength of the towels, use scissors to cut 3-inch (8-cm) x 12-inch (31-cm) strips from each brand of paper towel. Attach one end of each of the paper strips to a yard or meter stick with masking tape. Place the ends of the meter stick on cardboard boxes, stacks of books, or other supports so that the towel strips hang freely as shown.
   Now clamp a spring-type paper clasp on the end of one towel strip. Use a short piece of flexible wire to make a hook, and attach this hook to one of the holes in the handle of the paper clasp. Now add washers, large paper clips, or other similar uniform weights to the hook as shown.
   Continue to add uniform weights until the towel rips. Record the number of weights supported by the towel just before it rips. Follow the same procedure to test the dry strength of all your towel samples.
2. To test the wet strength of the towels, cut strips of each brand as you did in number 1 above. Then immerse each strip in a glass of water and place the strips in the same testing setup you used for dry strength testing. Record the number of weights each brand of towel will support when wet.

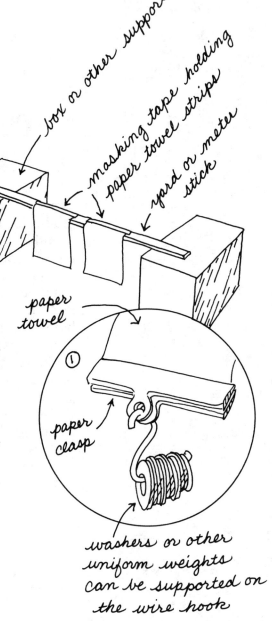

box or other support
masking tape holding
paper towel strips
yard or meter stick
paper towel
paper clasp
washers or other uniform weights can be supported on the wire hook

3. To compare water absorbency of the towels, you will need to build a simple balance scale. This can be done with a yard or meter stick, string, and two paper cups set up like this. Take samples of each brand of paper towel and use a ruler to measure equal-sized squares of each (12 inch x 12 inch or 31 cm x 31 cm might be a convenient size). Trim the samples with scissors until they are identical in size. Weigh each of these towel samples on the balance scale and record this information. Then, immerse all towel samples in water. Take each sample out of the water in turn, drain it for 1 minute, and weigh it. Record these weights. Do the following calculations to determine the amount of water absorbed by each sample.)

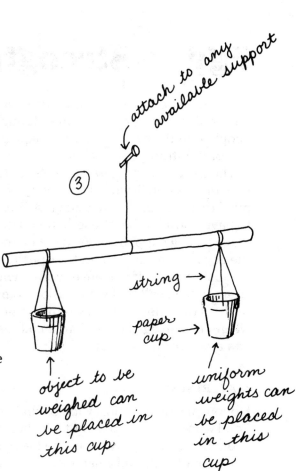

wet weight − dry weight = amount of water absorbed

4. To determine the scrubbing durability of each brand of towel, take one towel of each brand, wet it thoroughly, and scrub in circles with the towel on a flat surface. Count the number of circles completed before the towel falls apart. (Be sure to rub with the same pressure and use rubbing circles of the same size for each sample.)
5. To compare the softness of the towels, place samples of each brand in identical paper bags. Do a softness survey. Have a large number of people (kids and adults) reach into each bag and decide which towel feels softest to their touch. (Don't let them see the towels.) Make a chart to record the results of your survey.
6. Consider the relative costs and test results for different brands of paper towels. Decide which brand is the best buy.

■ INVENTIVE SIDETRIPS

1. Try to think of other qualities or characteristics of paper towels that were not tested. For example: Can it be recycled or reused? Does it leave lint? Design a method for testing the characteristic you think up.
2. Collect samples of different brands of some other product, such as flashlight batteries, glue, tape, seeds, lollipops, soap, pencils, plastic bags, or sponges. Invent a testing program and determine the best buy.
3. Analyze some of the scientific tests used by T.V. or magazine advertisers to sell their products. How valid are the testing procedures used? Make a collection of commercials or advertisements you believe to be examples of deceptive advertising.
4. Try to formulate some regulations you think the government should enforce to insure protection of consumers from inferior or worthless products.

Egg-O-Strength Tester

Hen's eggs are thought of as delicate and fragile perishables to be handled with care at all times. It might be surprising to many people that the basic structural shape of an egg—the dome—is one of the strongest known to architectural engineers.

The trick to demonstrating the structural strength of an egg is to avoid sudden jarring of the shell—if weight or pressure is applied to an egg and increased gradually, the egg will be found to have considerable strength. If you don't believe it, try this: Place an egg cupped between your hands so that the ends of the egg rest on your palms. Now push . . . really push hard to try to crush the egg. If you are endowed with average human strength, you will find it impossible to break the egg (unless you push on the sides of the egg—then it's easy!). Just how much weight can an egg hold before it collapses? Here is a device you can assemble to find out.

MATERIALS

Hollow plastic tube (just wide enough to accommodate an egg)
Solid wooden cylinder (about 8 inches or 20 cm long and of a
    diameter that easily fits inside the plastic tube)
1 or 2 small nails and a hammer
Piece of plywood about 5 inches (12 cm) square
Plasticene or other pliable modeling clay
Fresh, uncooked egg
Weights (stones or metal washers will do)
Food or baby scale

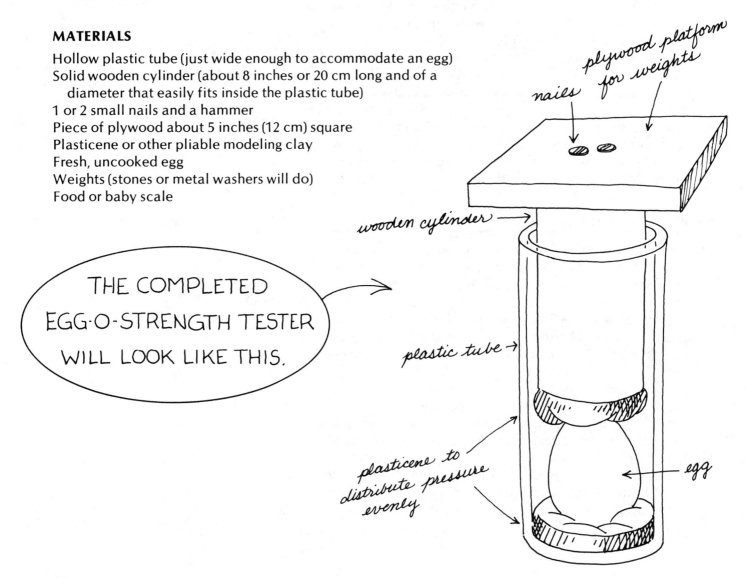

THE COMPLETED EGG-O-STRENGTH TESTER WILL LOOK LIKE THIS.

nails
plywood platform for weights
wooden cylinder
plastic tube
plasticene to distribute pressure evenly
egg

CONSTRUCTION

1. Find a plastic tube large enough to accommodate an egg standing on its end. (Some supermarket items are packed in plastic jars that are ideal.) Find or whittle a wooden cylinder that fits loosely inside the plastic tube. (Chunks of balsa wood available at hobby shops can be easily carved to make a suitable cylinder.)
2. With two small nails, attach a small wooden square to one end of the wooden cylinder. Stick some Plasticene to the other end.
3. Place the plastic tube on a firm base (a table or the floor) and put some Plasticene inside the tube's base. Place an egg on its end inside the plastic tube.
4. Gently lower the end of the wooden cylinder into the tube until its Plasticene-tipped end makes contact with the egg.
5. Add weights to the platform in small increments until the eggshell cracks. Stones or metal washers can be used for weights (these objects can be weighed later on a food or baby scale).

■ INVENTIVE SIDETRIPS

1. Find out if several eggs of the same size and weight all have the same weight-bearing strength.
2. Which is stronger—a raw egg or a hard-boiled egg? Do some testing and find out.
3. Do brown eggs and white eggs differ in their shell strength? Use the Egg-O-Strength tester to find out.
4. Can eggs be coated with any substance that will make them stronger? Try some experiments to find out.
5. Test the weight-bearing strength of other objects—ping pong balls, peanuts, Christmas ornaments or whatever else you can think of.
6. Invent a method that will enable you to do a product test to determine whether medium, large, and extra-large eggs actually differ in size and weight.

Rube Goldberg Contraptions

Rube Goldberg is well remembered for his cartoons of odd-ball inventions. Goldberg was a successful cartoonist who published many popular comic strips in newspapers and magazines. His most famous cartoon character was Professor Lucifer Gorgonzola Butts, the genius who demonstrated the inventions that eventually resulted in a Rube Goldberg being defined in *Webster's Dictionary* as "a device or method to accomplish by extremely complex and roundabout means a job that actually could be done simply."

A look at the following Rube Goldberg invention will reveal exactly what the dictionary means:

SIMPLIFIED PENCIL-SHARPENER

PROFESSOR BUTTS GETS HIS THINK-TANK WORKING AND EVOLVES THE SIMPLIFIED PENCIL-SHARPENER.

OPEN WINDOW (A) AND FLY KITE (B). STRING (C) LIFTS SMALL DOOR (D) ALLOWING MOTHS (E) TO ESCAPE AND EAT RED FLANNEL SHIRT (F). AS WEIGHT OF SHIRT BECOMES LESS, SHOE (G) STEPS ON SWITCH (H) WHICH HEATS ELECTRIC IRON (I) AND BURNS HOLE IN PANTS (J). SMOKE (K) ENTERS HOLE IN TREE (L) SMOKING OUT OPOSSUM (M) WHICH JUMPS INTO BASKET (N) PULLING ROPE (O) AND LIFTING CAGE (P), ALLOWING WOODPECKER (Q) TO CHEW WOOD FROM PENCIL (R) EXPOSING LEAD. EMERGENCY KNIFE (S) IS ALWAYS HANDY IN CASE OPOSSUM OR THE WOODPECKER GETS SICK AND CAN'T WORK.

Rube Goldberg started his cartoon inventions during the early part of this century when there was great interest in the development of new time-saving inventions. Looking around, he noticed that many of these time savers managed to complicate life in other ways. The famous Rube Goldberg contraptions were thus introduced to make people laugh at themselves and their gadgets and not take new inventions too seriously. At the same time, Goldberg was celebrating the marvelous creative abilities of humans. Though he poked fun at modern inventions, Rube Goldberg secretly had great admiration for the creative spark demonstrated by inventors.

Kids can have fun and at the same time exercise their creative abilities by inventing Rube Goldberg-type contraptions. Activity sheets featuring several such challenges are provided on pages 80–81. Teachers may duplicate the activity sheets for classroom use.

■ INVENTIVE SIDETRIPS

There are unlimited possibilities for creating Rube Goldberg contraptions. Using junk and readily available materials, try to build a humorous invention that will accomplish a task. Here are some ideas:

Build a device that would automatically:

☐ Crush an ice cube

☐ Crack an egg

☐ Mash potatoes

☐ Toss dice

☐ Turn pages in a book

☐ Trap a fly

☐ Remove the pit from an olive

☐ Make people laugh

☐ Clean muddy water

☐ Light a candle

☐ Water a house plant

☐ Wake you up in the morning

☐ Remove shells from peanuts.

Or, devise a task of your own and build a device to accomplish it automatically.

Inventors Notes and Solutions

This section of the **Inventors Workshop** provides some hints, solutions, and helpful information for problem solving in various activities and inventive sidetrips. Keep in mind that these notes do not provide the answers to challenges, but just possible solutions or approaches that might inspire another inventor to come up with another invention.

Inventive Sidetrips

A number of Inventive Sidetrips follow every project in **Inventors Workshop.** Some of these challenges are tricky, requiring some additional knowledge as well as the ability to problem solve. If an inventor finds him- or herself stumped on a particular sidetrip, here's the place to find extra helpful information or a suggestion for how to approach or think about the challenge that will inspire a solution. If an inventor has already successfully met the challenge of an Inventive Sidetrip, he or she might want to check out these notes anyway—for comparison's sake.

THINGAMAJIGS

Here is the solution to the pictures on the activity sheet for this Inventive Sidetrip (see page 75):

    Picture A—Foot Warmer
    Picture B—Butter Churn
    Picture C—Hat Tipper

WATER-EXPANDING MACHINE

1. To adjust the machine to apparently change water to a different liquid, simply place Kool-Aid powder, food coloring, orange juice or some other additive into the machine's internal reservoir. Water poured into the machine will then combine with whatever is in the reservoir, and the combined materials will flow from the output tube of the machine.

   If you want to add some fizz to the liquid produced by the machine, add half a cup of vinegar to the water poured into the machine, and one or two teaspoons baking soda into the machine's reservoir. When the vinegar and baking soda mix together in the reservoir, they chemically react to form carbon dioxide gas bubbles (exactly the same kinds of bubbles found in soda pop).

2. The trick to the illusion machine, of course, is to figure out some way to secretly switch a handkerchief for one of a different color, rocks for a sample of sand, or a red ball for a white ball. Try to develop a secret compartment or switching mechanism inside your mysterious contraption that can make the necessary exchange.

SMOKE RING MACHINE

1. You also might experiment with larger and smaller holes to see if you can find an optimum size for smoke ring formation.
2. You should be able to make dust rings as well as smoke rings. However, the smoke rings are longer lasting because smoke particles are much smaller than dust particles and they float in the air better.
3. Be sure to take safety precautions when starting a fire inside the box. Make sure any burning materials are completely extinguished when you are done.

MYSTERIOUS X-RAY MACHINE

1. Try putting smoke or dust inside the shoe box. Also, try making sketches with felt-tip markers on transparent glass or plastic and place these between the mirrors inside the shoe box.
2. Be sure to take safety precautions so you don't set the shoe box on fire. You may be able to create the illusion that the inside of an x-rayed object is burning.

CANDLE-POWERED STEAMBOAT

1. Try more than one candle or perhaps a can of Sterno solid canned heat as your heat source. If they are available, experiment with larger or smaller oil cans. Pinch the opening of the oil can stem to find out if a smaller opening changes the steamboat's speed.
2. If a good head of steam is produced by sufficient heat, this boat may move faster than the original one.

CANDLE-POWERED STEAM ENGINE

1. Add graphite or oil to the supporting bearings to reduce friction, use more or less water or change the size or shape of the turbine vanes. You could also pinch the opening of the oil can's spout to increase the speed of the steam.

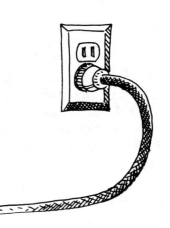

AUTOMATIC CANDLESNUFFER

1. A factor you might consider is that a candle loses weight as it burns. Could the loss of a certain amount of candle weight cause a seesaw motion to move the candle into a snuffer? Could water be dumped on the candle in some way? If an inflated balloon were popped, could the sudden rush of air be used to blow out a candle?
2. A wooden match can be caused to burn by striking it against sandpaper. You might attach a wooden match to a pivoting arm that is activated by a spring or rubber band to rub the match against sandpaper and deliver the flame to the wick of a candle. A long string might activate this device.

CANDLE CAROUSEL

1. Try more candles, longer sails, differently shaped sails, or whatever else you can think of.
2. If paper clips are too heavy, try small aluminum foil disks made with a paper punch or sequins as weights.
3. You can reverse the direction of rotation by reversing the bends in the sails and repositioning the candles under the newly formed bends.

ELECTRICAL SWITCH

1. To make a liquid that will conduct electricity, add salt to water until no more salt can be dissolved.
2. To work, a bulb holder must connect one wire from a circuit to the metal side of the bulb and another wire from the same circuit to the metal tip of the bulb, as shown.
   This enables electricity to flow through the wire pathway inside the bulb and make the filament glow.
   A paper clip, two brass paper fasteners, and a small piece of cardboard can be used to rig a bulb holder as shown:
3. The switch described in this activity could be used as the trip mechanism. Wire this switch into a circuit with flashlight batteries and a buzzer. When a cat steps on the switch, the buzzer will sound. (Suitable battery operated buzzers can be obtained from Radio Shack and other electronic supply firms.)

STEADINESS TESTER

1. To do this, simply replace the flashlight bulb and holder with a commercially made electric bell or buzzer. You may need to add more batteries to the circuit to have sufficient voltage to operate the bell or buzzer. (Bells and buzzers that operate on direct current from flashlight batteries are available from Radio Shack and other electronics supply stores.)
2. You also might want to investigate the relative steadiness of the same people at different times of the day. (People may be steadier in the morning when they are more rested and more alert.)
3. Here is one way to solve this challenge.

MAGTRON THE MAGNETIC MARVEL

1. Some possibilities are: a) connect thread to Magtron's flag and find a way to use this moving thread to make a paper or aluminum doll dance up and down; or, b) attach a small hammer to Magron's flag so that he can ring a bell as he moves up and down.

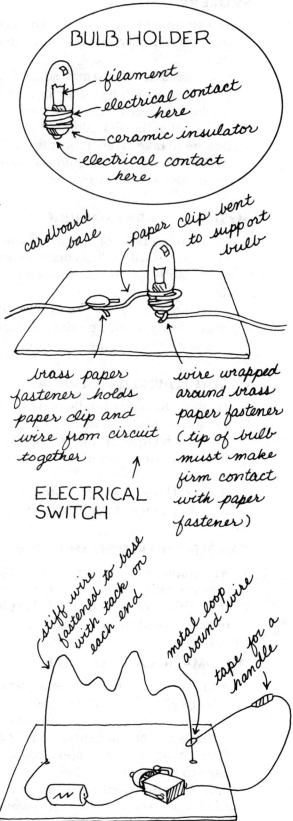

BULB HOLDER
filament
electrical contact here
ceramic insulator
electrical contact here

cardboard base

paper clip bent to support bulb

brass paper fastener holds paper clip and wire from circuit together

wire wrapped around brass paper fastener (tip of bulb must make firm contact with paper fastener)

ELECTRICAL SWITCH

stiff wire to base fastened with tack on each end

metal loop around wire

tape for a handle

STEADINESS TESTER

2. You may be able to cause Magtron to dive more energetically if you use more flashlight batteries or more coils of wire. If you reverse the current on the electromagnet (by turning the battery around), Magtron will jump instead of dive.

MAGNETTA THE MAGIC DANCER

1. You might add more flashlight batteries to the circuit, improve the strength of the electromagnet by adding more coils of wire, or attach some small permanent magnets to Magnetta's feet.

MONSTER BUBBLES

1. Plastic pipes and tubes of all sizes are good, as are funnels, plastic soap or bleach containers with bottoms removed, and some toy horns and whistles.

2. One way to make a bubble inside another bubble is to first make a large bubble (actually a half bubble) by blowing through a straw into a saucer full of bubble soap solution. After the large half bubble is formed, simply leave the straw in place and blow another smaller bubble inside.

3. Kids can try adding food coloring, various dyes, and tempera paint to soap bubble solutions. They will find it impossible to render any significant coloration to bubbles. This is because of the extreme thinness of the soap bubble's film—the film is so thin that the small amount of dye it contains is not visible to the human eye. When sufficient coloring material is added to the soap to make the thin layer visible, there is not enough soap left to form a bubble!

4. Long lasting and fairly durable bubble sculptures can be made if gelatin is added to the glycerin and soap bubble solution. Dissolve a package of unflavored gelatin in 10 ounces (300 ml) of boiling water, and use this instead of the plain water for the basic bubble solution recipe given in the activity. (Stir the other ingredients into the gelatin water solution after the gelatin has completely dissolved.) It is best to keep this mixture warm over hot water in a double boiler on a hot plate or stove. Small amounts of this bubble sculpture solution can be dispersed to kids in styrofoam cups. Gelatin bubbles are tough skinned, will adhere to each other, and keep their shape.

5. Bubbles can be caught intact, and even bounced, on synthetic carpet materials. There are two reasons for this:
a) the bubble solution does not easily wet the synthetic fibers; and, b) the bubble and the carpet material tend to have the same electrostatic charge, thus weakly repelling each other.

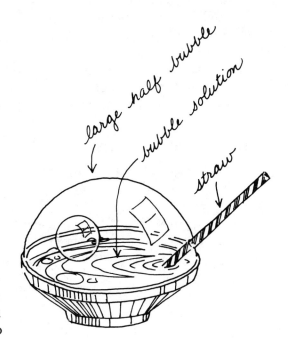

large half bubble

bubble solution

straw

BUBBLE-MAKING MACHINE

1. Try larger circles of wire on the bubble wands.
2. Large plastic rings can be sliced from styrofoam cups and attached to the bubble wands.
3. You might try attaching pieces of wire or plastic mesh to the machine's bubble wands.
4. The crank could be turned by a wound up rubber band or by dropping a weight attached by a string wound around the axle of the crank.
5. When vinegar and baking soda are mixed they chemically react to form harmless carbon dioxide gas. Could you devise a contraption engineered to use this gas to blow bubbles?

TOOTHPASTE DISPENSER

1. Rubber bands could be rigged to keep roller pressure on the toothpaste tube as shown.

cement ring here

②

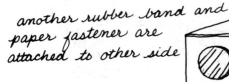

another rubber band and paper fastener are attached to other side

①

rubber band

brass paper fastener to anchor rubber band

2. One way to do this is to cement a cardboard or plastic ring to the side of the toothpaste dispenser as shown.

WATER CLOCK

1. You also may want to compare the accuracy of your home-made clock with that of a commercial stopwatch. The time increments of your water clock may change slightly as the level of water in the reservoir changes.
2. See the activities on circuits and switches if you need some ideas as to how you might do this. These activities are Electrical Switch, Steadiness Tester, Magtron the Magnetic Marvel, and Magnetta the Magic Dancer found on pages 29–38.
3. Salt can be used instead of sand to build some sort of hourglass. An hourglass sand clock can be fashioned from two narrow necked glass jars separated by a piece of cardboard or plastic with a small hole in it.

    Pendulums make accurate clocks because the time increment for a pendulum bob to make a complete swing is always the same, even when the pendulum begins slowing down (the bob moves faster when it swings farther, slower when it moves over a shorter distance).
4. See the activity Invention Dissection on pages 8–9 for more help with this challenge.

③

sand or salt in glass jar

tape plastic with hole in it around neck of one jar, then tape jars together

DISCO LIGHT SHOW MACHINE

1. A small electric motor from an Erector Set or an old barbecue rotisserie might be used. Or, a windup motor from a toy might do it.
2. One way to do this is to insert small finish nails to the turning dowel inside the machine and position some flexible metal strips near the dowel so the nails hit the strips as the dowel turns (the principle of a music box). Another possibility is to attach bells or chimes to the turning dowel.

OPERATION EGG DROP

1. Marshmallows could be used as packing material surrounding an egg or they could be glued on the outside of an egg package.
2. Inflated balloons could be tied to form a protective package around the egg.
3. You might consider paper or cloth streamers, a parachute or some sort of airfoil (wing).
4. You could build a frame of toothpicks or soda straws around the egg. The frame should be large and weak so it collapses on impact.
5. You could incorporate a rubber band powered windup propeller on your package that would act like a helicopter rotor, thus slowing the descent of the package. Attach the rubber band to the inside of the package and to a dowel that is attached to the propeller. Wind up the rubber band by turning the propeller. When released, the rubber band will rotate the propeller. You could also consider installing model airplane or model rocket engines into your super egg package to slow its fall.

PROJECT EGG LOFT

1. Virtually any package designed for Operation Egg Drop could be adapted for use in Project Egg Loft.
2. Your catapult might be energized by a large rubber band cut from an automobile or truck inner tube.
3. The flying bat or delta-wing type of kite is excellent as an egg-carrying kite.
4. You might consider building a spring-loaded cannon to solve this challenge.
5. Kits are available for model rockets that include payload compartments large enough to accommodate an egg. These model rockets are normally engineered to soft land on terra firma by aid of a parachute, so they are excellent solutions to the Egg Loft Challenge. Remember to follow all safety instructions accompanying the rocket.
6. If you do this at school, you may want to get some local

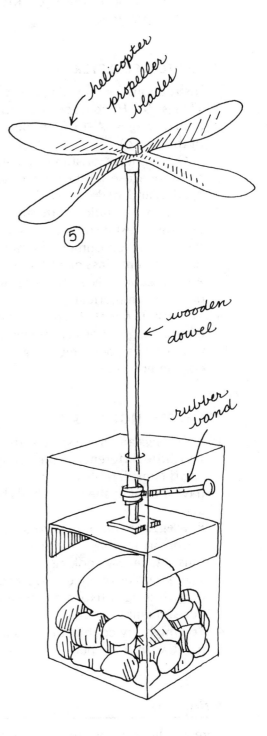

helicopter propeller blades

⑤

wooden dowel

rubber band

PAPER TOWEL TESTER

1. Instructions for recycling paper are available in *Making Things: The Hand Book of Creative Discovery* by Ann Wiseman on pages 14–15. (Complete reference is included at end of this book.)

   Other characteristics which might be tested are a) flame resistance (use safety precautions); b) oil absorbency; c) odor; and, d) dry strength.
2. In a school situation, different groups of youngsters might choose to test different types of products, and present their results at a "consumer information conference" presented to a different class or a PTA meeting.
3. A tape recorder is useful in collecting sound tracks from T.V. or radio commericals.
4. Youngsters might also be interested in finding out what government regulations are currently in existence regarding control of drugs, foods, electrical appliances, and other consumer products.

EGG-O-STRENGTH TESTER

1. If the eggs are in the same state of freshness there will be very little difference in their weight-bearing strength. If an egg is considerably older than others, however, it is likely to have a weaker shell. The shells become more brittle as they age.
2. Raw eggs are normally stronger, especially when they are fresh. The reason is that eggshells are made more brittle, and thus weaker, by cooking.
3. There is no difference in average strength of shells of brown and white eggs. (Nor are there any differences in the nutritional qualities.)
4. You might try coating the eggs with various types of glue, paint, varnish, or plaster.

Solutions

Here are the solutions for the Mysterious Pushrod Box problems and the Absolutely Ridiculous Eating Utensils. The Pushrod Boxes are discussed in the text on pages 12–13 and shown on the activity sheets on pages 77, 78, and 79. The Ridiculous Utensils were inspired by Rube Goldberg's inventions (see pages 62–63) and may be found on the activity sheets on pages 80 and 81.

MYSTERIOUS PUSHROD BOXES

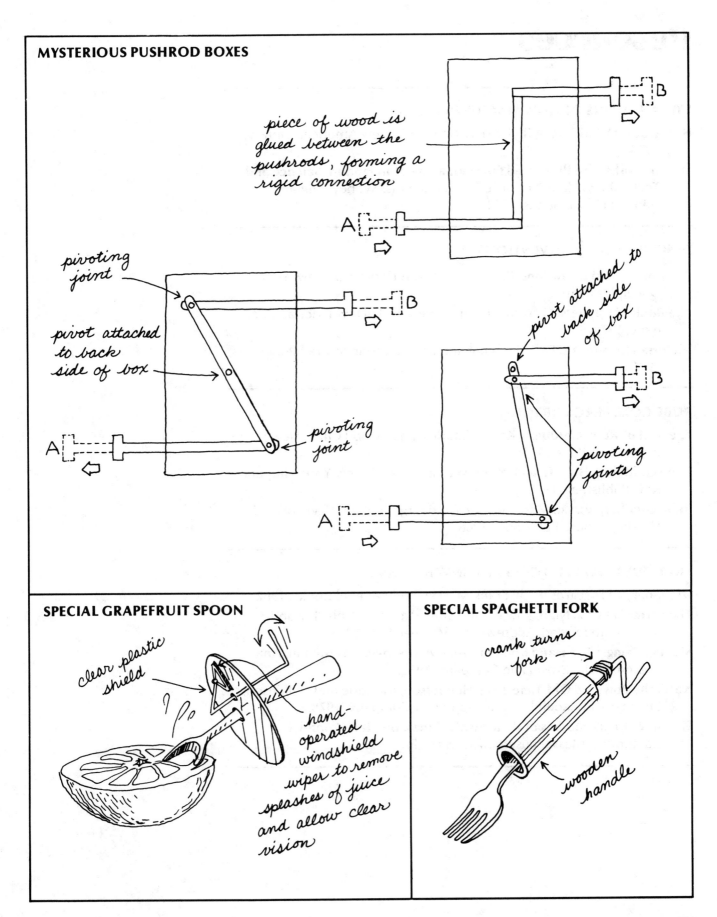

piece of wood is glued between the pushrods, forming a rigid connection

pivoting joint

pivot attached to back side of box

pivoting joint

pivot attached to back side of box

pivoting joints

A

B

SPECIAL GRAPEFRUIT SPOON

clear plastic shield

hand-operated windshield wiper to remove splashes of juice and allow clear vision

SPECIAL SPAGHETTI FORK

crank turns fork

wooden handle

Resources

EXPLANATIONS OF HOW MACHINES WORK

How Does it Work? Koff, Richard M. New York: New American Library, 1973.

How it Works: The Illustrated Encyclopaedia of Invention, Science and Technology. Hamlyn House Editors. 20 vols. Sydney, England: Hamlyn House Books, 1974.

DESCRIPTIONS OF INVENTIONS

Absolutely Mad Inventions. Brown, A.E. and Jeffcott, H.A. New York: Dover Publications, 1970.

The Book of Gadgets. Grossinger, Tania. New York: David McKay Company, 1974.

Victorian Inventions. De Vries, Leonard. London: John Murray Publishers, 1971.

RUBE GOLDBERG CARTOONS

The Best of Rube Goldberg. Keller, Charles. Englewood Cliffs, New Jersey: Prentice-Hall Inc., 1979.

Rube Goldberg: His Life and Work. Marzio, Peter C. New York: Harper & Row Publishers, 1973.

Rube Goldberg vs. the Machine Age. Goldberg, Reuben. New York: Hastings House Publishers, 1968.

MORE IDEAS FOR PROJECTS AND INVENTIONS

Dictionary of Discards. Rich, Frank M. New York: Avenel Books, 1962.

The Formula Book. Nigh, Edward and Stark, Norman. Vols. 1, 2 and 3. Kansas City: Sheed, Andrews and McNeel, Inc., 1978.

Making Things: The Hand Book of Creative Discovery. Wiseman, Ann. Boston: Little, Brown and Company, 1973.

Naturally Powered Old Time Toys. Henderson, Marjorie and Wilkinson, Elizabeth. Philadelphia: J. B. Lippincott Company, 1978.

Simple Working Models of Historic Machines. Burstall, Aubrey F. Cambridge, Massachusetts: The M.I.T. Press, 1975.

Potato Possibilities

Below are some of sketches of plain old raw potatoes. Just for fun, and as an exercise in imagination, take a pencil and draw details in and around each potato sketch to convert it to something else. See the example at the right.

Try to make as many *different* objects as you can (not all automobiles, for instance) and try to come up with the most unusual modifications of the potato sketches that you can.

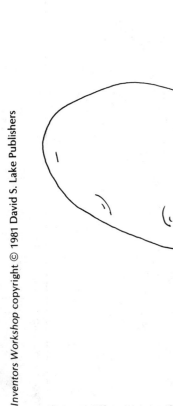

73

Combine and Conquer

List of objects:

_____   _____   _____

_____   _____   _____

_____   _____   _____

Combined, these objects can _____

_____

Sketch:

Real Thingamajigs

Here are drawings of three thingamajigs that were actually given U.S. patents—or were actually manufactured! In the spaces below each picture, write down the possible uses the gadget might have had.

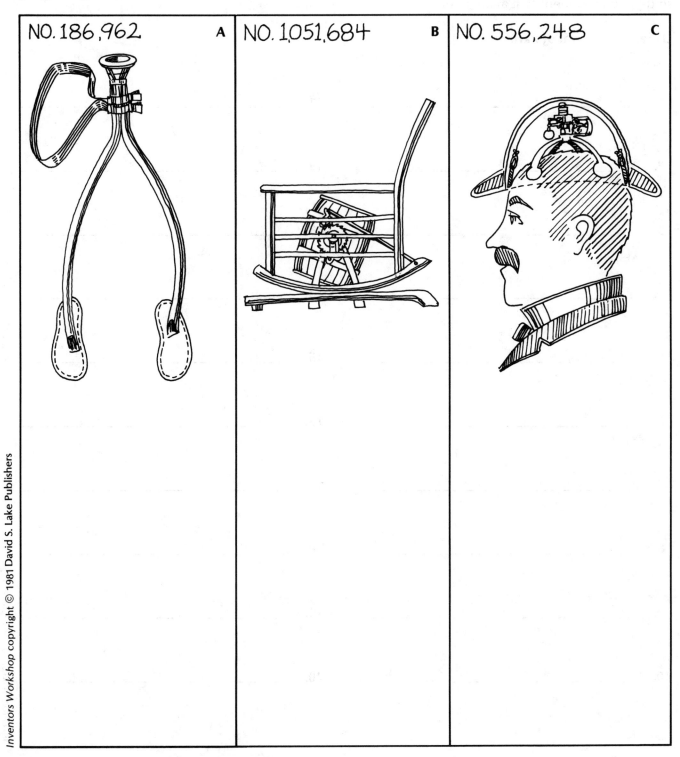

NO. 186,962   **A**

NO. 1,051,684   **B**

NO. 556,248   **C**

Invention Dissection

As you proceed to take a mechanical device apart, make a list of each part and the order in which you removed it. Then you will be able to put the machine back together again more easily. If you don't have a name for the part, draw a rough sketch so that you can identify it again later.

Order of Removal of Parts

1. _____
2. _____
3. _____
4. _____
5. _____
6. _____
7. _____
8. _____
9. _____
10. _____

11. _____
12. _____
13. _____
14. _____
15. _____
16. _____
17. _____
18. _____
19. _____
20. _____

Pushrod Box Problem 1

Operation: When Rod A is pushed in, Rod B moves out exactly the same distance Rod A is pushed in. When Rod B is pushed in, Rod A moves out an equal distance.

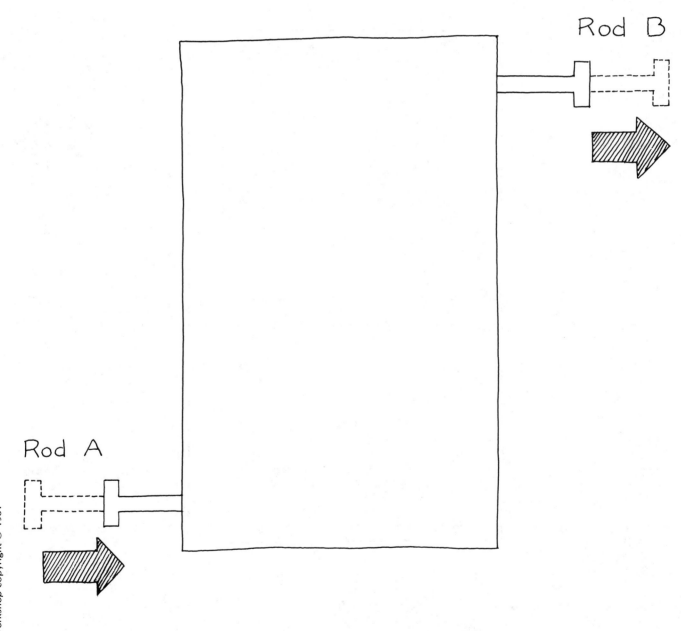

Pushrod Box Problem 2

Operation: When Rod A is pulled out, Rod B moves out also and to exactly the same distance as does Rod A. When either of the rods is pushed back in, the other rod moves in also.

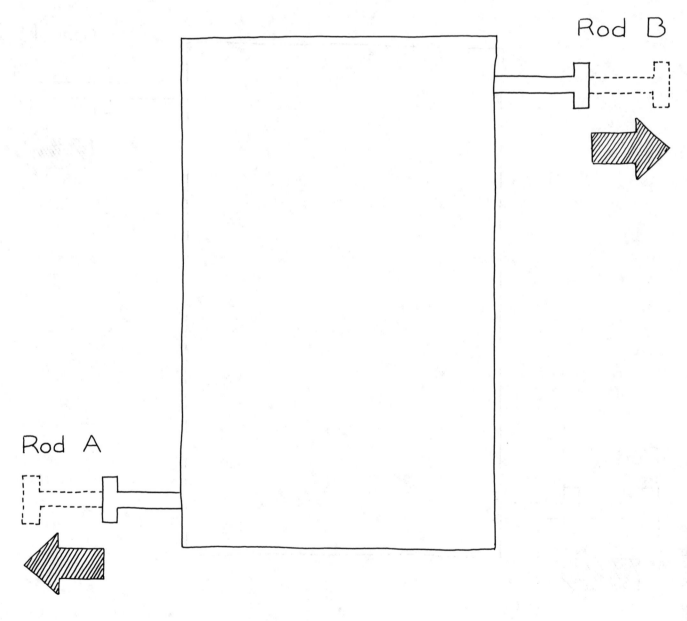

Inventors Workshop copyright © 1981 David S. Lake Publishers

Pushrod Box Problem 3

Operation: When Rod A is pushed in a long distance, Rod B moves out a short distance in the same direction. When Rod B is moved out a short distance, Rod A responds by moving a long distance in the same direction.

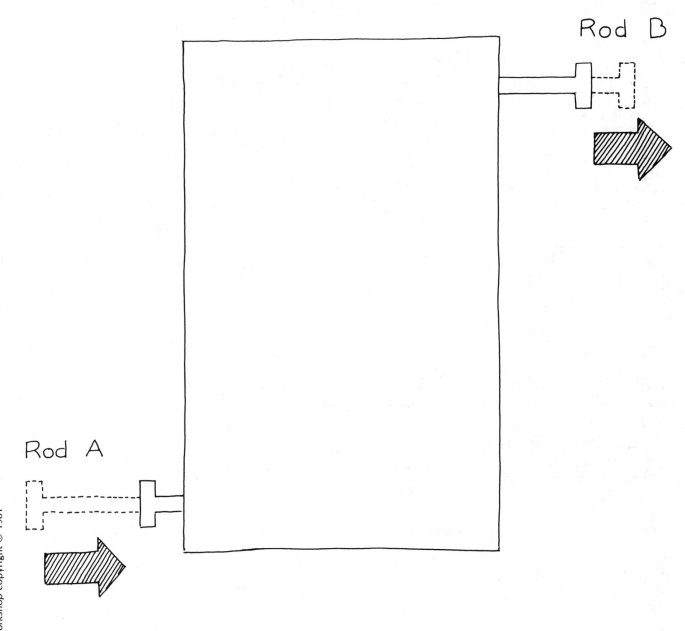

Absolutely Ridiculous Eating Utensils

Problem: When you eat chinese food, the noodles slip off your chopsticks. Here is a Rube Goldberg type solution to this problem.

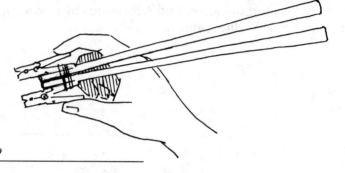

TITLE *non-slip chopsticks*

Now, it's your turn. Make some sketches of some crazy ideas for eating utensils to solve the following problems:

Problem: Grapefruit juice squirts in your eye when you dig sections out of your grapefruit with a spoon. Make a sketch of an oddball or humorous solution to this problem.

TITLE _____

Problem: You have trouble winding up spaghetti on your fork. Draw a Rube Goldberg type solution to this problem.

TITLE _____

Inventors Workshop copyright © 1981 David S. Lake Publishers

Automatic Balloon Popper

Sandra, a sixth-grade student, was inspired by Rube Goldberg's cartoons to design her own crazy contraption useful for popping balloons at parties. Here is her invention:

Now it's your turn. Design and build your own Automatic Balloon Popper. You might want to reconstruct Sandra's balloon popper before you build your own. In any case, make your popper as complicated and as humorous as possible, in the true tradition of Rube Goldberg.

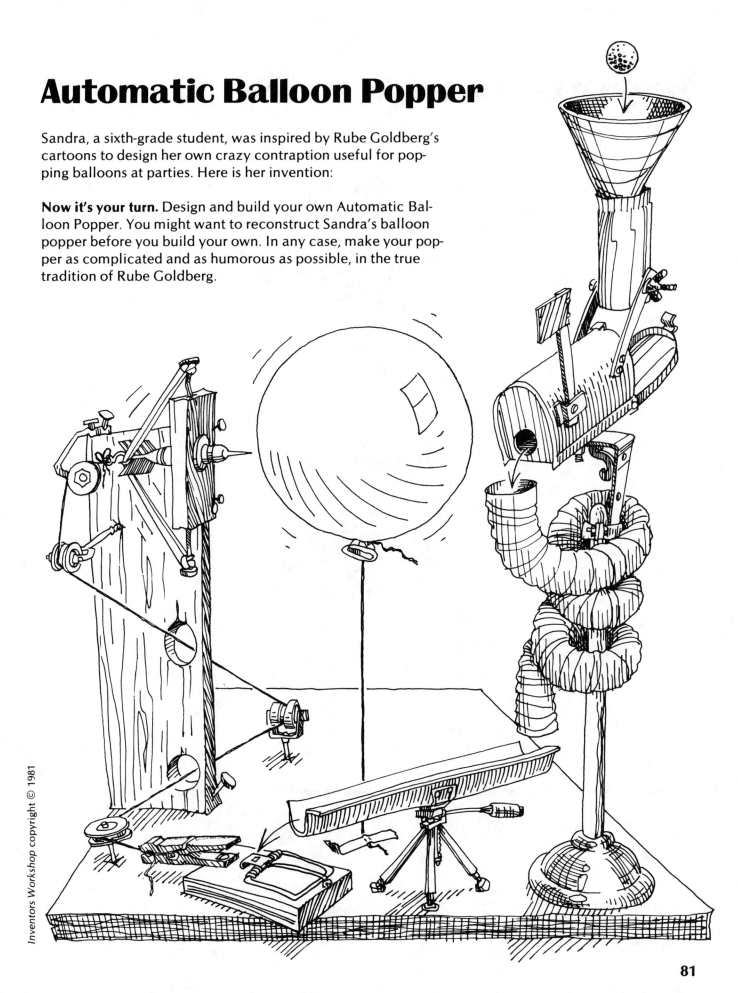

Magnetta the Magic Dancer

Inventor-at-Work Signs

Inventor-at-Work Signs

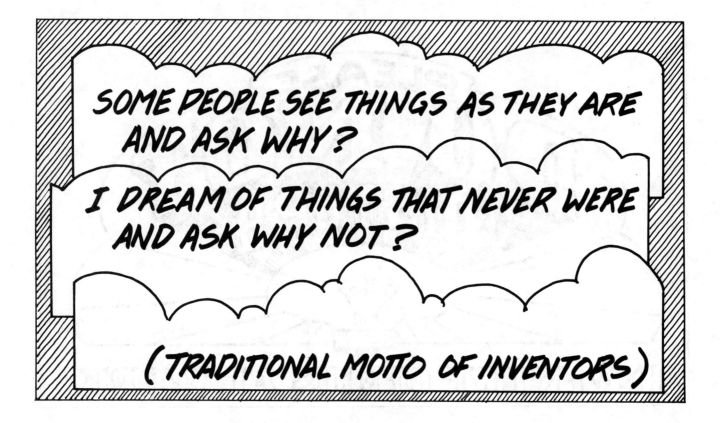

SOME PEOPLE SEE THINGS AS THEY ARE AND ASK WHY?

I DREAM OF THINGS THAT NEVER WERE AND ASK WHY NOT?

(TRADITIONAL MOTTO OF INVENTORS)

DON'T LAUGH

THIS INVENTION MAY CHANGE THE WORLD